SUCCESS LEAVES TRACES

SUCCESS
LEAVES TRACES

An Incredible Method to Change Your Life By
Embracing Little Known Mental Strategies
Designed to Create The Life You Deserve

ARMAND MORIN

NEW YORK

LONDON • NASHVILLE • MELBOURNE • VANCOUVER

SUCCESS LEAVES TRACES®

An Incredible Method to Change Your Life By Embracing Little Known Mental Strategies Designed to Create The Life You Deserve

Published in New York, New York, by Morgan James Publishing. Morgan James is a trademark of Morgan James, LLC. www.MorganJamesPublishing.com

ISBN 978-1-60037-878-2 paperback
ISBN 978-1-60037-879-9 eBook
Library of Congress Control Number: 2010939556

Morgan James is a proud partner of Habitat for Humanity Peninsula and Greater Williamsburg. Partners in building since 2006.

Get involved today! Visit
MorganJamesPublishing.com/giving-back

DEDICATION

To my Mother and Father, this book represents the beliefs and ethics you instilled into me whether you knew it or not. My success in life is a direct result of the life you've given me. I've never said it, but thank you, and I love you very much.

To my children, Anthony and Avery, both of you are my "reasons why." Each and every day of my life, I work to try to be an example of the person I hope you to be. I love both of you more than words can say.

Last but not least, my wife, Marianna. You've always stood by my side from the very beginning. Without you, I could not have achieved anywhere near the level of success I've had. You're my wife, my lover, my partner and more importantly, you're my best friend. I'll love you forever.

ACKNOWLEDGMENTS

I don't want this book to go without acknowledging the people who have played a big part in making it happen, specifically the best team anyone could ask for, Marianna Morin, George Callens, Frank Deardurff and Bill Smith.

Plus a very special thank you to Chris and Jim Howard for working endless days editing and piecing together my thoughts in a coherent manner so people can understand what goes on in my head.

Thank you to David Hancock and the Morgan James publishing team for all your hard work to making this book a reality.

To all of you, thank you for what you do and helping me make this book become a reality. Now get back to work!

TABLE OF CONTENTS

Dedication v

Acknowledgments vii

My Story 1

Introduction 39

Element One — Observation 43

Element Two — Sequence It 55

Element Three — Amplification 65

Element Four — Who 73

Element Five — Timeline 81

Productivity 93

Change 107

Belief 121

Stop Factor 131

Super Self 149

Opportunity Matrix 165

Epilogue 185

About The Author 187

MY STORY

"Ever since I was a child I have had this instinctive urge for expansion and growth. To me, the function and duty of a quality human being is the sincere and honest development of one's potential." — Bruce Lee

There I was, steadily pacing back and forth wearing away a path in the carpet, just moments before walking out onto the stage to speak in front of more than 7,000 people at the O2 in London. "You can do this. It's no big deal. You've spoken in front of thousands before, and you did great. Why are you so nervous now? Just remember, be yourself and what happens, happens."

These were just a few of the many thoughts going through my mind at that moment. Was I nervous? You bet I was. I don't know too many people who wouldn't be. Over 7,000 people waiting to hear from me; it was shocking and almost surreal.

The stage crew was running all around ensuring everything would go as planned. The make-up person was working on me so I wouldn't look pale on stage in front of all the lights. She made some small talk as she applied the make-up. I just smiled. I wasn't really hearing her. All I could think of was whether this stuff would run if I start sweating under the lights. Boy that would just look horrible. I took off my sport coat to try to keep cool before I walked out on stage. "Never let them see you sweat." I had I heard that before. Well, that wasn't going to work for me today and there was nothing I could do about it.

That day wasn't one of the smoothest in my life. My family, my team, and I were in London for several days prior to the event getting prepared. It's not every day you speak at the O2 in London, and we wanted everything to go just right.

I woke up that morning feeling pretty good about everything. I took a shower, dried off and went to the closet to take out my suit. I pulled the pants out first. I put them on and at that very moment DISASTER STRUCK LIKE LIGHTING!

OH NO! I'M SCREWED!

Let me give you a little background. Just a few days earlier I had purchased, a brand new suit. I normally purchase suits off the rack because I'm a pretty average size, and I've never had any problems doing this before.

This time I did have a problem, and it was a pretty big one.

Apparently, as I was trying on different size pants, I accidentally put the WRONG ONE BACK!

My pants didn't fit. They were too small—way too small.

Think about this. On one of the most important days of my life, my pants don't fit, and I don't have a spare suit. To make matters worse, I don't even have time to go back to the store and get the right size.

So, what did I do?

I did like any man would do in that particular situation. I PANICKED and yelled for my wife, Marianna.

Marianna rushed into the room knowing something was definitely wrong. I rarely get nervous and almost never panic. In fact, I don't think she has ever actually seen me in panic mode. I told her my dilemma with tears in my eyes like a child who just lost their dog.

I could see the sympathy and the "oh crap" look in her eyes all at the same time.

Thank God, my wife acted very swiftly and calmed me down.

She proceeded to tell me jeans and a sport coat is in style and that it would separate me from all the other speakers at the event. It would make me look more relaxed. I knew what she was doing, trying to make good out of a bad situation. I tried to convince myself she was right, and I think I did a pretty good job of selling myself on it.

I nervously joked about it with everyone I met that day.

Back at the O2, my intro is playing and I'm getting ready. The curtain rises, and I walk out ready to speak as if nothing ever went wrong.

But...

The big story you want to know is how an average half Filipino, half American guy who literally grew up on the wrong side of the tracks, with nothing more than a high school education created a business and a lifestyle normally reserved for those of with a background of privilege and wealth.

- How did I figure out what many people never find their whole life?

- Was it some secret book or tablet?

- Did a dying billionaire mentor me?

- How did I go from drop dead broke to building one of the most successful direct marketing companies in the world almost entirely on a shoestring budget?

Friend, that is exactly what the book in your hands right now is all about.

It's my story and more importantly, what I've learned and the system I've pieced together over the years which has gone on to teach thousands of people from all walks of life that SUCCESS LEAVES TRACES if you know where to look.

No, I'm not going to regurgitate what you've probably heard over and over again. I'm sick of reading and hearing the same old crap too.

Crap like…

- Manifesting your way to millions
- Thinking positively will change your life
- If you believe in it strong enough, it will happen

Cute sayings like these are fine but at the end of the day, they are just words.

You'll quickly learn that I'm very straightforward with my opinions, and I'm not afraid to tell you them, just ask me.

Trace #1 - Stand Up For Something! Have an opinion.

Mr. Miyagi from the Karate Kid said it best. "Walk on this side of road, OK. Walk on that side of road, OK. Walk in middle of road, squished just like grape."

What I believe and what I've discovered is that success in life and in business is a science, not just any science but a very precise and exact science. It's one that can be duplicated in any facet of your life. Much of what I will show you is designed with business in mind, but every single element of this system can be and should be applied to your personal life, as well. Whether it is your health, finances or relationships, these methods still work and will work wonders if you take the initiative and apply them.

I call it a science because it's NOT guesswork. It's a series of processes. Each one is powerful on its own but once combined in a certain specific sequence, the results are nothing less than astonishing.

Once learned, you can and will be able to achieve success in absolutely anything you choose to do. You name it, and you'll be able to do it. Whether you'll want to do it is an entirely other story.

So who am I?

Chances are, you've never heard of me.

You see, I'm what I refer to as "selectively" famous. If you go on the Internet and do a search for my name "Armand Morin," you'll find it on literally millions of websites.

I've had dinner at Buckingham Palace with Prince Charles, met celebrities all over the world and I have even had a charted Billboard Magazine Album. In fact, the album at one point was #7 in all of the world on the Internet charts.

Yet, I can walk down the street, and no one will ever notice me.

Like I said, I'm "selectively" famous. If you are not involved with online marketing, then I'm a total stranger to you, but not for long.

So let's start from the beginning.

I believe to truly understand an individual; you must know where they came from. Like most people, I have a very unique story and every little piece of it is important. It all has a role in how I developed the system, which I'm about to teach you as you read this book.

So again, who am I?

My name is Armand Morin and this is my story…

I grew up in a small town in upstate New York. We lived in Massena, a fairly small rural town of around 20,000 people. It wasn't known for much except for the St. Lawrence Seaway and the Thousand Islands. We basically lived on the Canadian border. In fact, so close that every year, we would all go over to the river on July 2nd, which is the Canadian equivalent to our 4th of July and watch the fireworks display in Canada. It was literally just a half-mile across to the other side.

Massena is a union town; most people worked in one of the three factories—Alcoa, Reynolds, or Chevrolet. Those were the three prevalent companies that employed not only almost all of Massena, but also the majority of the North Country in New York at the time. These days, many of these plants closed or near closed due to downsizing.

When I was maybe four or five, my father was fortunate enough to get a job working for Alcoa, the largest aluminum company in the world. In Massena, this was the epitome of having a good job. You had steady employment, paid vacations, health and dental insurance, the whole works. To most people, this was a dream job.

His job, though, was working in what was called the "pot rooms." This simply meant he worked exactly where the aluminum was made in extremely hot temperatures all year round and he had the fun experience of having molten aluminum splash up on him every now and then. It wasn't a glamorous job, but it kept a roof over our head.

We rented much of the time when I was young. The first house my parents bought was just $2,500 through a foreclosure sale. It was a built in the late 1800's and needed a lot of work, but it was a great deal, especially for a family just starting out. I lived in that house until the day I moved out to venture on my own.

On a side note… the attic in that house scared me silly. You had to get down on your hands and knees to crawl through this little hole into what seemed to be a huge room to a little kid. It was about 20'x30'. One small window and no lights made it even eerier. It didn't help that my older brother had told both my younger brother and me about an old lady haunting that place. I still have never paid him back for that.

Back to my story…

Dad had job security, a union, the whole works, and that was great. The one thing I noticed, though, was that he always kept trying to achieve something bigger and better. As I was growing up, I didn't understand why, but as I learned the importance of money in society I completely understood. My father also knew that there was a better life out there, he just didn't see the traces in front of him to achieve it.

As I am writing this, it's hard NOT to notice an opportunity in what I just said. You see, I've now trained myself to see opportunities in almost everything I look at. I just mentioned a moment ago that my father purchased our home at a tax sale for only $2,500. What if he would have realized that he could do this over and over again? Was it a missed opportunity? I would say yes.

I think we need to go back a little further to let you see the full story. You see, my father met my mother while serving in the Vietnam War. Yes, I call it a war. I don't know what else you would call it when thousands of people die for their country. These people deserve the respect of it being a called a war and not a just a mere conflict.

My mother is from the Philippines and grew up quite poor which is basically the norm for most people in that country. Coming to the USA was definitely a culture shock for her in more ways than one. Not only did she leave her family and move half way around the world, she moved to upstate New York where the cold winters would make an Eskimo shiver.

My dad always knew there was something else; he knew there was a better life; he knew there was a possibility of him actually getting some of it, but he just didn't know how to make a difference.

This is your first lesson. Money is NOT power. Knowledge is power. Specific knowledge. You can have all the money in the world, but if you do not have the knowledge of what to do with it, you'll soon be broke again. With proper knowledge, you achieve great wealth. Combine this knowledge with desire, and you have a winning combination and formula for success.

No matter how many ideas and investments he came across, tried, and eventually gave up on, he never gave up trying to find that one thing that would work for him and that would create a change in his life and in our family's financial situation.

He tried different things, but he lacked the knowledge of what to do; he knew he could do better, he just didn't know how to make "better" happen for us. You see, making a difference requires certain knowledge. He tried and tried, and nothing worked out the way he anticipated, but he didn't give up on his dreams. Whether he knows it or not, this one lesson is probably more responsible for my success than anything else.

Here are some of the things that he did:

- Have you heard of a program called Merlite Jewelry? It's a catalog program that has costume jewelry. He had this little case, I remember it being in our closet, and it had rings in it and some watches, earrings, and stuff like that. He sold some, and that was good, but it wasn't a successful venture.

- He bought into SMC. It's been around forever. It's a program where you buy these wholesale products and then sell them. He got the SMC manual for around $20 and sold this stuff from it. The program made him *some* money. In fact, it was really interesting how he did it. What he did was took the products to the nursing home around Christmas, where my mom had a job at the time. They would set up tables and sell products there. He let the customers come to him, which is actually a valuable lesson that I learned.

- He also tried network marketing, Amway, and he really didn't make any money in that, but I learned from this venture the importance of concept I call success by association. The whole concept was to uplift people to achieve their desires. I can't put into words how much I learned my simply observing his participation in this.

He tried several ventures while I watched, observed, learned, and I saw him doing different things in order to make a difference for us. I took note of what seemed to work, what didn't, and why things would fail or succeed. My father didn't become rich in any of his investments, but whether he knew it or not, he taught me some valuable lessons, and I will now pass some of them on as you follow the steps I took to success.

I don't know if my father knows it or not, but I wouldn't be where I am today if it wasn't for him instilling the idea that opportunity exists. For that, Dad, thank you.

My father always told me, "Get an education." I can't tell you how many times I heard this over and over and over again. I can still hear it to this day. "Don't be like me and have to go to work in that dang factory all your life. Get an Education!!!" I have to laugh looking back, because he usually ended his rant with a little bit of fear… "If you boys ever get a job at Alcoa, I'll personally kick your butts."

He was only half right, though.

You have to understand this about my father. He had an 8th grade education and moved around a lot when he was young. My grandfather always moved to where the jobs were. There was no other choice. My father quit school to go to work to help provide for his family. My guess is that my father looked back and figured that his missing education was one of the key elements of him not going further in life.

We've all been brainwashed to believe that formal education is the key to success. But has that really worked for the majority of people out there? We all know very well educated people who are flat busted broke.

You see, what I've learned about education is that there are two types of education.

1.) School or formal education

And what I would call...

2.) Practical education

Before I get a flood of calls and emails about this, let me state a fact. I am all for formal education. I believe it will make you a well-rounded person and give you the ability to function as a human being. I will certainly encourage my children to go to college, but I do realize it's not what you learn in the classroom that matters most.

But... I'm sure you knew this was coming. Formal education will not necessarily make you rich. You see, I've become a great student of the wealth creation process. Of all the great success stories in history and in the world, formal education did not play a major part. Sorry, but it's true!

- Einstein absolutely hated school. He was even held back.

- Bill Gates quit college.

- Edison had a 3rd grade education.

- Henry Ford was not educated and was even taken to court for "ignorance." He won, by the way.

- Some a little more contemporary, like Facebook's Mark Zuckerberg quit college.

I could go on all day on this. My point is not to downplay education, but to let you in the secret of the ultra successful. The secret is this. Practical education is key to unlocking the door to anything you want.

Here's a basic principle, if you want to know how to do something. You could go to school and learn how to do it yourself. It may take weeks, months or years. Why waste all that time? The majority of what you will be doing is studying theory or general concepts, which brings up one of my big pet peeves. When learning a theory, most people take it as gospel. NO, NO, NO. A theory is just that a theory. It hasn't been proven to be true yet. Yet, a certain percentage of the population will waste precious time implementing theory as fact.

Back to my point, if you want to know how to do anything in the world, simply find someone who is already doing it and do what they do. It's simple, saves time and more importantly, it works.

As I mentioned earlier, at the time my father discovered, tried, and eventually moved on from money making ideas that led to dead ends; we didn't have a lot of money, but we weren't the only ones.

Our town was made up of people like us who were hard working, blue-collar citizens.

There were basically two classes of kids at school, poor like me, and the rich kids that lived on a place that most people referred to as "Hamburger Hill." The area was dubbed "Hamburger Hill" because its residents mortgaged themselves to death, and all they could afford to eat was hamburgers. Okay, maybe they could afford it, but many people referred to is as this to justify their place in life. Have you ever done that?

I guess you could say we weren't any different from the rich kids, they just had nicer things. Their "richness" was all flash, show, and they lived above their means, while we lived lives we could afford. As a kid, I didn't realize my life was already rich. I wanted what they had, and I didn't realize they were living beyond their means till later. I longed to be one of those kids on the other side of the tracks. I literally lived three houses across the tracks, and it was hard not to desire the lifestyle they had.

On television I saw lifestyles I wanted to live as well, like on *Lifestyles of the Rich and Famous*. "Hi, this is Robin Leach, and this is *Lifestyles of the Rich and Famous*." Do you remember that show? That caused you to dream quite a bit, didn't it? I would sit in front of the TV and say things like "Man, I'd love to have that house. That would be great! How much? Five million dollars? Get out of here!"

At around the same time, shows like *Miami Vice* with Don Johnson in his perfectly tailored white suit and pink shirt, driving fancy cars through scenic Miami were popular. I thought, "Yeah, I want that! I want that lifestyle." Those guys had the cars, the money, the girls, and they had a gun. Maybe that's how they got the money, the car, and the girl. However they got it, I wanted what they had.

By watching TV and my neighbors on "Hamburger Hill," I saw this lifestyle that I knew was available. I knew there was more to life than what I was experiencing. I knew that some people had found the key to that lifestyle that my father had been searching for throughout my youth. Obviously, someone was experiencing it somewhere, and I decided to go to college so I, too, could live that lifestyle and one day become rich and famous.

I'll never forget the first time I saw my first multi-million dollar home in person. Oddly enough it was in the Philippines. Every five years my father received a 10-week vacation. When I was 13, we went to the Philippines to visit my mother's family.

My mother had worked for a family called the Venegas. They were definitely rich. I remember pulling up to the house with huge 15-foot fence around it with armed guards at the top of the towers. We walked into the house, and it had marble walls and floors. Mrs. Venegas walked us into her husband's study. He was away on business in Paris at the time. He was very active in the Rotary Club and had one whole wall full of awards from them.

She pulled out a gift she had purchased for her husband. I'll never forget it, a Presidential Edition Rolex watch. Diamonds circled the face and the gold was almost blinding. At the time, that specific Rolex cost $25,000. That was 10 times the price of our house. Needless to say, it left a lasting impression on me as did the whole experience.

As I finished high school, I looked to do what any person of that age did—go on to college. On my way to riches, I went to college for business administration in Poughkeepsie, New York. "Why business administration," you ask? Because that is what all the tests I took told me I should do. While in college, I met a teacher by the name of Bruce Cassel.

Bruce Cassel was a little different than most teachers I had. He had real life experience. I believe he was also a business consultant on the side. I remember one example he told me. He would charge people $100 to register their businesses with the county. It was pretty slick because it cost only $25 to register your business at the courthouse downtown. The client filled out the form, gave him $100 and he literally walked it over to the courthouse for a cool $75 profit. It taught me that people are willing to pay for knowledge.

Mr. Cassel told me two important things I will never forget:

- Go buy the book called *Think and Grow Rich*
- If you don't know how to do something, pay someone else to do it

These were things that I had never heard before, and since I was determined to become rich and wealthy, I decided to take his advice, and he was right. *Think and Grow Rich* did change my life. I've probably read it about once a year since then, but that first book I bought is still the most special in my library.

The closest bookstore that sold it was five miles away. Because I didn't have a car, and I was too shy to use the public bus systems, I literally had to walk five miles to get that book.

Did you catch that? I was too shy at that point in my life to use public transportation. You see, in the small town where I grew up, we didn't have public transportation like that. I didn't know how to use a bus, and I was too timid to ask anyone. I would also have to say embarrassed too, embarrassed that I didn't know how. This kind of clues you into my frame of thinking at that time in my life.

I'll never forget that day. It was in the middle of September in 1988, one of the hottest summers ever in New York. At that time it was extremely hot, probably close to 100 degrees and there I am on the side of the road walking five miles one way, just to buy a book.

Not just any book—the book that possessed all the secrets to success.

It was the book that was responsible for more millionaires than any other book in history, the book that would unlock my true destiny for wealth and let me not want for anything else in my life forever more.

As you can tell, I was fired up and excited about getting my hands on this knowledge the wealthy have kept secret and closely guarded all these years.

Once I arrived at the bookstore, sweaty, tired, dehydrated, and even more glad to finally have made it, I walked over to the bookshelf, fumbling through all the books. There it was, a little white paperback with green letters peeking out between the other books almost screaming for me to pick it up.

I bought it and walked right back out in the heat, threw out the wrapping and the bag, and during the entire five-mile walk home, I read the book feverishly with a passion. I couldn't put it down. I was looking for the big secret to be revealed to me. I spent the rest of that day reading that book. I even skipped classes the next day to finish the book.

I walked a total of 10 miles to get the book, spent two entire days reading it. I didn't leave my little, one-room apartment until I read it studiously from cover to cover. After I was finished, I sat back on my bed in my 280 square foot apartment and said… "I don't get it." I'm serious! I didn't get it. Nice read, nice story, but how was it going to help me make any real money? I didn't put it all together at the time. I kept the book though, and didn't realize until many years later the significance of the information and how to apply it to my life.

When the student is ready, the teacher will show himself. I don't know who said that but I do believe it is true. I wasn't ready for that particular information yet, although I did absorb much of it.

After my experience with the book and skipping class to read it, I started skipping classes more and more. The reason I did this was because I was thinking, "These people aren't making any money. They're trying to teach me how to be successful, how to go out in the real world and they're not making any money, or at least making what I would call real money." A salary of $20,000 or $30,000 a year didn't appeal to me. I wanted to make millions. "This doesn't make sense to me." So instead of going to class, I started going to the library. I knew I just needed the right knowledge, and I wasn't going to get it in class.

I spent all my days in the library reading books on real estate and investing, and the funny part is that I don't do anything involving real estate to this day, but I've read almost every single book there is on the market that has been written on the subject. Then something strange happened.

The girl I was going out with at the time asked me to stay down south after the first summer. We were both from Massena. The only reason I went to school in Poughkeepsie was because she went to school in New Paltz about 10 miles away.

I knew if I went back to Massena for the summer, my best chance at a job would be about $4.00 an hour or so. That wasn't going to cut it. Not after I had been exposed to the big city life. I knew I could get a much better, higher paying summer job right where I was.

Needing a job, I did like any other person would do. I bought a newspaper and pulled out the help wanted ads. That was where I saw it—the perfect job for me. It read something like this...

> Success oriented people wanted
>
> No experience necessary
>
> Unlimited income potential
>
> Call: XXX-XXX-XXXX

I called the number and a man picked up with a heavy New York accent. He asked, "What do you do?" I said, "Well, I'm a college student. I'm going back to school in the fall, and I need to make some money. He said, "Perfect! We have a college program. Come in and see me tomorrow at noon."

I drove 20 miles to get to this amazing interview. When I drove up to the address. I had to look twice to see if I was at the right place. What I saw almost put me in shock. Imagine a building with an enormous 30' tall giant size vacuum cleaner sitting on top of it. *Do you think I was excited at that moment? Would you be excited?*

Visions were going through my mind with men in plaid suits with big fat cigars talking fast and shoving vacuum cleaners down people's throats. It was definitely NOT for me. I was destined for greatness and selling vacuum cleaners was never mentioned in *Think and Grow Rich*.

The girl I was dating at the time went with me, and I looked at the vacuum cleaner, turned to her, and said, "I'm not going in." She said, "You've got to go in." I asked, "Why?" She looked me straight in the eye and said, "Because you made an appointment, and you have to keep it." I shook my head and said, "I'm not selling vacuum cleaners." She nodded and said, "Yes, you are." She won.

I got out of the car and went inside. I wasn't happy about it, but she was right. I did make an appointment, and I had to keep my word to show up. I guess there was a pattern developing of following advice, whether I wanted to or not.

The man I was introduced to was the greatest salesperson I've ever met, even to this very day. His name is Lenny Epstein. He was from the Bronx, New York. Lenny sat me down and told me, "We've got a college program for you; you can make all this money." I said, "If I can make all kinds of money, count me in." He smiled and said, "Be here tomorrow morning at 8:00 a.m. Oh yeah, here are two pieces of paper I want you to memorize, and make sure you wear a tie." I took the papers, and said, "Good enough. I'll see you tomorrow."

What Lenny just showed me was that I could make as much as $30,000 over the summer selling vacuum cleaners. I was shocked. That amount of money might as well have been a million dollars. My father had to work all year to make that, and I could do it in only two months. This was definitely for me, only one small problem. I didn't own a tie.

The interview was on a Sunday, and I was to show up on Monday ready to work. We were living in New Paltz, New York at the time, which was a very, very small college town. If you think you've heard of it, it's probably because it was mentioned one time in the movie Dirty Dancing. That's about the only reference most people would know about.

Nothing was open on a Sunday in New Paltz except the second hand thrift store. I had no choice. We went in and believe it or not, the only tie they had was a bright red bow tie. What are the chances of that? Yes, a big fat bright as a clown's nose, red bow tie. To make matters worse it was a clip on. I looked like a waiter at a bad restaurant, but at least I would have a tie as I was told.

I followed Lenny's advice and went home and memorized what he gave me. *Why?* He told me to do it. I grew up in a small town, and if someone told me to do something, I had better do it. That was a very important step in this process. I was able to follow directions.

You need to be able to follow directions. I want you to write that down. Write, "I need to be able to follow directions." It's an important part of your success process.

The paper was a sales script. Two pieces of paper contained the whole sales presentation.

When I walked into the office the next day, Lenny asked me if I had memorized the paper. I said, "absolutely—100%." He put me to the test and made me recite word for word the entire presentation. What I found odd was that he was amazed and almost shocked that I actually did it. What he didn't tell, and I wouldn't find out until much later, was that NO ONE ever memorized the presentation. Hmmm.

Lenny said, "Armand, you're going to go out with this guy named Elliott Spiro." Elliott was a real nice guy with a heart of gold, who lived up on Hunter Mountain. Elliott was also kind of a celebrity, as well. He invented video greeting cards. You might remember them in the early 80s—nice videos with holiday music playing in the background. He did well until his partner ran off with all the equipment and left Elliott hanging with nothing. Now Elliott sold vacuum cleaners, go figure.

I went out with Elliott. We had two appointments to see people. The way the program worked was telemarketers would contact people to have their carpet shampooed for free if they would also allow us to show them the vacuum cleaner. It was a sweet deal for the customer and the odds were good that after seeing the vacuum cleaner and what it did, they would buy it.

We went on two appointments and sold four cleaners—two vacuum cleaners, and two shampooers, in two different houses. He then told me, "Here, put your name at the bottom of this." I asked, "What's this for?" He said, "You just made these two sales." I shook my head and said, "No, you made these two sales." He insisted, "No, you made these two sales," so I agreed and signed my name.

At the end of the day (I didn't want to be too presumptuous or anything like that), I asked, "How much money am I going to make?" He answered, "Well, you've made about $600." You've got to realize, the most money I had ever made in a week was $140, and I made $600 on two appointments in one day, and it seemed too easy. I was willing to do anything for $600 a day.

I had a big shock coming. I went to work the next day and guess what happened? No one was in the office. The office was bare. Everyone was gone except for one person, and that was Sue, our secretary. They didn't tell me after we came back to the office the day before that the rest of the office had won a trip to Hawaii, and they were going to be gone for the next seven days. I said, "Well, what am I supposed to do?" Then Sue looked at me and said, "Well, they told me to tell you to go out and knock on doors." No one showed me how to knock on doors. This was not in the script. I had no clue what to do or what to say to the people who opened the doors. I asked, "What am I supposed to say?" She said, "Well, just say who you are, and tell them you're from Electrolux." (That was the name of the company.) I said, "Okay. I can do that."

Scared does not even come close to the feeling I felt that day. Remember, a few months before I wouldn't even ride the public bus system and not much had changed since then. They wanted me to walk up and down the street and talk to strangers all day. I wasn't too excited at this point or motivated to get going very fast.

I did go out, determined to earn another $600. I drove around looking for the PERFECT neighborhood, one that looked like the residents would have money to purchase the vacuum cleaners and one that looked like a friendly place. After four hours of driving around, I came to the conclusion that the PERFECT neighborhood didn't exist.

Let's stick with the perfect neighborhood story for a minute. Isn't that what many people are doing right now? They're driving around looking for the perfect neighborhood, looking for the perfect opportunity? *Have you ever done that, waited and looked for the perfect opportunity before you got started? Or looked for the perfect conditions?*

Let me tell you this—it doesn't exist, just like *my* perfect neighborhood didn't exist. As I was driving, I didn't realize that I was procrastinating because quite honestly starting something new can seem a little overwhelming at times. Maybe you've never knocked on doors, but I'm sure you've had a similar experience before. Four hours is a long time to drive around neighborhoods!

Selling vacuum cleaners door to door goes against everything my mother had taught me growing up.

- Never talk to strangers. (It's necessary in sales.)
- Don't ask strangers for money. (Sales are based on this.)

Direct sales is one of the most if not the most lucrative opportunity in the world, but we have all been trained since infants on exactly how not to do it. It isn't any wonder why the majority of people who attempt a direct sales career fail. It's not their fault.

After I realized I would not find what I was searching for, I finally got out of the car and got up enough courage to knock on a door. No one told me the hardest door to get through would be the one on my very own car. I went ahead and knocked on the first door. The person answered, and I said, "Hi, my name is Armand, and I'm from Electrolux. I'm in the area, and I was wondering if you need anything?" You have to remember, I didn't even know if they even owned an Electrolux vacuum cleaner.

Surprisingly they said, "Yes I do. I need some bags. Do you have any bags?" So far, so good... I smiled and said, "Yes I do." I went to the car, got some bags, and I sold her a package of bags. I made seven dollars off that sale. I was happy! Seven bucks, that would normally take me over an hour to make, and I made it in just a few minutes. I started thinking, even if I don't sell a single vacuum cleaner, I could make a great living just selling bags. I was always the optimist.

Then I went to the next house and anticipated my approach would have the same outcome. So I asked the same question again, only this time she said, "No." The first door slammed in my face. You know, it wasn't so bad.

I went to the next house went through my very clever sales pitch and she also said "No." Maybe I wasn't cut out for this. Elliott made it look so easy yesterday.

I didn't stop though, I've only made seven dollars and that wasn't nearly enough for a good days pay and certainly a far cry from the $600 I made the day before. So I continued on to the next one and she said, "Well, my Electrolux isn't working." I said, "Gee, you should probably get that fixed. Let me take a look at it." *What did I know about vacuum cleaners? This was my second day!*

Luckily I was observant in the office the day before, and I saw the repairman do something which I just repeated. I have to tell you how I did this because it's really funny. I walked inside, looked at the vacuum cleaner, opened it up, took the bag out, and ran my hand up along the inside of it. I said, "Boy, this looks pretty dirty." Of course it was dirty; my hand was on the inside of a *vacuum cleaner!* She said, "Wow! There's that much dust in there?" I said, "Yeah, there is. I can take it in for you, and we can have someone take a look at it." She said, "Yes" so I wrote it up. I took it in and got it fixed for her. They had to do some work on it. By the end of that first day, I'd made about $100. Not bad from just knocking on doors.

This was a 100% commission job. If I didn't sell anything, I didn't eat. Now that's motivation.

The next day I walked into the office and low and behold, I was informed by our secretary that I didn't have to knock on doors. I had two new appointments. Boy, was I relieved.

I went on my first appointment with my script all memorized, and I was ready to recite it at the drop of a dime. I was ready for another $600 day. I could just feel it.

When I got to the house, my nerves were getting the best of me and I basically just started vacuuming without saying a word. The whole time I was sweating profusely knowing I should be telling the lady of the house my well rehearsed sales pitch. I was blowing it in a big way.

Finally she broke the ice. Probably knowing I was extremely nervous or maybe she just didn't want me to sweat all over her house. She asked me, "Where are you from?" I said, "I'm from a small town in upstate New York you've probably never heard of called Massena." She said, "I'm from Malone!"

If you're not familiar with upstate New York, Malone happens to be the next major town east of Massena; it's only about 30 miles away. We were almost neighbors. At that point she and I both opened up and started talking. Unknowingly and mostly by luck, I had created a rapport with this lady. Yes, she did end up buying.

I didn't realize it then, but she liked me, and that was the key to earning her business.

No one can teach you how to develop rapport. At that time, all I knew was; in business, you have to be yourself.

People say, "Fake it until you make it." That is the biggest load of crap I have ever heard in my life. If you fake it until you make it, all you do is turn yourself into a big fake. *Am I right?* If you practice to be a fake, you ultimately become a fake.

You don't want to be a fake, you want to be real. You want to be honest. You want to be the person who you are, not the person who someone else wants you to be.

After a period of time, it just wasn't working out with Electrolux, so after two years, I decided I would find a better job; something more established with more prestige, or so I thought.

The first time I answered an ad in the paper, I ended up getting a job, so why not go right back to the paper and look again. And that's exactly what I did. I picked up the Sunday paper since that had the biggest selection and started looking.

And then I found it...

Here's what the ad said...

Success oriented people wanted

No experience necessary

Unlimited income potential

Call: XXX-XXX-XXXX

Hmmm… that sounded familiar. I called it anyway. They immediately told me it wasn't Electrolux, so I went in for the interview. I arrived with about 30 other people at a hotel. A well dressed gentleman started talking about opportunity with this company and that it was owned by Berkshire Hathaway and was a Warren Buffet company. This sounded pretty impressive. I could see myself working for Warren Buffet, who wouldn't.

Then he brought out the product. A Kirby Vacuum cleaner! I couldn't believe it. My mouth dropped. Oh no, here we go again. I can't get rid of vacuum cleaners. But, you have to understand I needed a job, I already knew how to sell vacuums, and it sounded like a good opportunity. I took the plunge into the dirty world of vacuum cleaners all over again.

This was different right from the start. My first trainer, Randy, was very smart. He knew that in order for me to sell this product, I had to believe in the product first. If I had any doubt that Electrolux was better, I would never be able to sell.

He took me aside for a whole day and we compared apples to apples. You could say we had a vacuum cleaner showdown. Who won you ask? Well let's put it this way. When I bought my most recent house, the first thing I did was call the Kirby guy to come over, so there's your answer.

That also brings me to another lesson. In anything you do in life, you must believe whole-heartedly in what you are doing or else you will receive meager results. If you don't believe it in it, then don't do it.

With Kirby, I had a great learning experience. They had selling down to a science. Here's what I mean. I was given a brochure with exactly 100 things to say to a prospect while in their home. I didn't have to think one bit. The claim was that if you memorized all 100 things, you could be a millionaire in five years with the company. It's a pretty strong promise. Did I memorize all 100? Well, I could get to about 87 or so just rattling them off the top of my head at any given point in time.

I was still able to close one out of every three people I showed the vacuum to even on a bad day. You may think this is a great closing ratio, but it was really just the national average. If you showed it three times a day, you should get one sale.

Whoever came up with their sales process was absolutely brilliant. Do this and say this and you'll get a sale. You just can't get any simpler than that. It was a system that had been time tested and had a proven track record. I wasn't special at selling. I just followed their system and I did it well. I simply followed instructions.

I worked for Kirby for the next three years. I did pretty well most of the time, but every now and then I would get into a slump and not sell anything for a week or more. Those were the tough times. In many cases I would have to put my tail between my legs and call home to ask for $20 or $30 to last me the week for food. I have to say, I hate Raman noodles to this very day because of it. Don't even get me started on spaghetti. I had my fill of that too.

This lesson leads me to the part of my story that caused a turning point in my life. As I got older, I met a girl, and we ended up having a child together. My son's name is Anthony. He's kind of like me, which is funny. He's a born salesperson; he really is. He closes me all the time.

I've got to tell you a story. Kids are natural closers. When my son was about seven years old, he called me on the phone and said, "Dad, I need seventeen dollars." "Seventeen dollars? What do you need seventeen for?" "Well, I have to buy some candy. I have to get film for the camera that you bought me, and I need this and that, I really need seventeen dollars." I said, "That's a lot of money." He said, "No, no, I need seventy-seven dollars." I said, "Seventy-seven dollars? You were just at seventeen dollars." He said, "Well, I need seventy-seven dollars. I forgot. I want to get two video games too." I said, "Oh no. I'll have to think about that one." He said, "Well, just forget the seventy-seven dollars, and give me the seventeen dollars." This is a true story! I was thinking, *"Oh my God!"* I felt so used.

When I first met his mom, I was still selling Kirby vacuum cleaners, only this time I was living in Vermont. After a certain period of time, I just didn't want to sell vacuum cleaners anymore. I turned back to old faithful—my trusty Sunday help wanted ads. Except this time I looked at it differently. I was going to be more strategic in my job hunting. If wanted a better job. I should get a better newspaper. So I upgraded my newspaper to the *Wall Street Journal*. Why not? This is where the most successful people would look and a better company would be, right?

I saw an ad, which sounded great. It was definitely another winner for me.

> Telecommunication Sales Reps Wanted
>
> No Experience Necessary
>
> Unlimited Income Potential
>
> Call: XXX-XXX-XXXX

Now I have to admit. I had no idea what telecommunications even was, but I didn't need any experience and I knew how to sell, so I called.

It was a company out of Chicago—Cherry Communications. I'll never forget the name. The man who answered the phone was the president of the company, and I was talking to him.

The first question he asked me was if I had any door-to-door sales experience. I responded in my most confident voice and said, "As a matter of fact, yes I do—VERY EXTENSIVE EXPERIENCE." I then proceeded to tell him about the last five years of my life selling vacuum cleaners. He said, "Perfect". Listen to what happened next.

He asked me for my fax number. Let me set the stage. At this point I had taken a small job as a telemarketer selling jewelry to beauty salons over the phone. I took the job because I had to have some sort of income coming in. It wasn't a great job by far. The idea was to get the salons to let us put our display of earrings in their salon. They would buy the display outright and keep all the profits.

As I said, I was calling in this broken down old building where the telemarketing company was. When he asked me for my phone number, I said, "Hold on." I picked up the phone book and looked up the nearest copy store. All copy stores have public fax machines, and I gave him that number. I didn't want to let him know that I didn't have a fax machine.

He faxed me over two pieces of paper. The first piece of paper was a contract to work for the company, basically stating what I would be earning. I was paid on a commission basis according to how big their phone bill was. The minimum I would make was $9.00 and if their monthly long distance bill was over $100, I was paid $60.

The second piece of paper was called an LOA. It was how I got paid. It stood for Letter of Authorization. If you signed this paper, it gave the company the right to switch your long distance bill to them.

Now, I was a full-fledged Telecommunications Sales Representative.

My job was to knock on residential doors and try to get people switch their long distance to us.

They didn't give me any training, just my LOA. So there I was with a piece of paper that I had to turn into money somehow. I sat down and had to do some brainstorming to figure out how to do this. I knew I could sell, but they didn't give me a system this time. I had to figure it out on my own. *What is the best way to do this? What tools would I need?*

One of the things an older gentleman at Electrolux told me was, "You're young, and if you want people to take you seriously, you'll have to dress better than them." So part of my toolbox consisted of suits and nice sport coats I had accumulated over the years. I already had that.

What else would I need? "Hmmm… I got it!" A clipboard, yes that's it. If you walk up to someone's house with a clipboard, it immediately change their perspective of you. You now are on official business. So I went down to the stationary store, near my house and bought a clipboard for $1.55.

The last thing I needed was something to say. I would figure that out as I went from door to door.

That night, I did the research on my new job. If I wanted to sell long distance, I should know something about phones. So I picked up the phone book and started reading all the information, which no one ever reads. I started on page one and read until the listings started. I tore out a few of the pages to carry with me for reference.

The next morning I woke up, excited and ready to get started on my first day as a Telecommunications Sales Representative. I walked out the door and walked up to the first street I came to and started knocking.

Slam, Slam, Slam, Slam and Slam. Needless to say, I wasn't doing too well. It seemed like everyone was literally slamming doors in my face. But with each house I tried a different approach. Edison tried over a thousand ways to make a light bulb work. I had only a few doors slammed, so I didn't take it personally.

Finally at about the 50th house, I got it right.

Here's what I said… Hi, my name is Armand and I'm asking people a few questions. Which of these services do you use AT&T, MCI or Sprint? What is your monthly long distance bill? Did you know you are paying XXX per minute for your long distance calls? Look this is right from your phone book. I would show them the pages I ripped out the night before. At that time, the phone book showed the per minute call rates for those three carriers. You could continue to pay XXX every month or you could save XXX. Which would you rather do?

That was basically my presentation. She said, "Yes!" I had my first sale. I repeated the process at the next house, and the next house. I signed up about six customers that day and made about $280. The best part is I didn't even leave my neighborhood.

After a week or so, I had a brilliant idea. I said why can't I have other people do this for me? I called up the president of the company and said, "You're paying me $9.00 for a small monthly bill. I would like to pay someone $4.50. It won't cost you any more money. I'll pay them out of my share. How could he say no?

I then put an ad in the paper that read like this…

> Success oriented people wanted
>
> No experience necessary
>
> Unlimited income potential
>
> Call: XXX-XXX-XXXX

Look familiar? It worked on me, I'm sure it would work for other people.

I rented a space at the town hall to hold interviews and about 20 people showed up. I told them the job and how it worked. About 10 of them said, "Yes." I met with them and handed them my script that I typed up. I made it easy for them.

To build belief the system worked, I would walk up with each one of them and recite the script word for word to get the sale. Once they knew I was reading the script, they were more apt to recite it word for word.

Here's a small lesson I learned when working with people; most people will only do 50% of what they see you do. It's true. So, show them twice as much to get them to do 100% of the job.

This worked for a while. I made out okay, but my problem was that I lived in a very rural area of New York and had to travel 30 miles to get to a major city where there would be enough houses to work.

Here's another bit of information about me and my youth. I was irresponsible. At that time, I didn't have a driver's license due to a few unpaid tickets and even a DUI. I am not proud of this. I was young and stupid, and I paid a price for it. With my son's mother working, I didn't have anyone to drive me around. I tried to make this happen, but it didn't really work for me. I was working an uphill battle. Yeah, I made money sometimes, but more often than not, I didn't.

Completely by accident, I picked up a telecommunications magazine one day and figured out the company I was working for was getting residual income from my sales.

They paid me only once, but they made money month after month off of these customers. I wanted some of that; get paid every month for the work you do only once. I'll talk more about this later on.

I decided right then and there I wanted it. I was going to start my own long distance company. I was going to go head to head with AT&T, MCI and Sprint. Why not? I had knocked on doors and sold long distance. I was certainly qualified. How hard could it be?

- What would be the obvious elements of a long distance company? You need telephone lines. I could get a contract for this.

- You need your own phone bill. This is basically paper with your logo on it.

- You need customer service. This could be outsourced.

That was really about it. It took months to get a contract with a company who let us do this. In my due diligence, I discovered that there was such a thing as a "carriage contract" with AT&T. This meant we use their lines, their customer service, their billing but we get wholesale rates.

The long distance rate at the time was $.35-$.40 cents a minute. I could sell and make a profit by selling it at only $.19 cents a minute. Needless to say this was great. I would sell their service for about half of what they charge.

Word started spreading about my new venture quickly even though it didn't even start yet. I only told one person, but I told them to keep it a secret. To make a long story short, my secret had a waiting list of over 500 people who wanted to sell our service for us, just based upon word of mouth.

After five months of working on this deal, no money was coming in, but we were close to getting a signed contract. I could see it happening. I just needed more time.

I always had this idea engrained in my head that you have to keep trying. This came from watching my father try for so many years. I knew that if it doesn't work the first time, you have to keep trying. Don't give up, just keep trying.

There is one day I'll never forget. It was in April of 1995, Easter Sunday, and there was a knock at my door. A guy showed up, moved out my son and his mother, and they were just gone. These are the words that she said as she left that day, "You'll never amount to anything. You're a loser. You're just playing at this business thing."

I had been working night and day for five months trying to develop a long distance company of my own. Like I said, it was going to work, I could feel it.

She said, "You're playing at this business thing. You're never going to amount to anything. We're gone. We're leaving." She had met some guy on the side, and she moved in with him and took my son about five hours away.

Now, thinking back, I really couldn't blame her too much. We didn't have any money; I was pretty much flat dead busted broke. I had no money. I had an apartment, luckily next door to my parents' house, and if it wasn't for my mom making a little bit extra for dinner, we wouldn't have survived as long as we did.

Sometimes when you get your back up against the wall, you have no choice.

One of the worst things I think people can have is too many choices, options, or things they can do. I had no options. There was nothing I could have done at that point except succeed or fail.

If I didn't succeed, that meant that she was right in leaving. She would have been right. But if I succeeded, then I was right. I was following that dream, the dream that I had, because I got to the point where I said, "This is it! This is it! This has to be it, because I have to have this! I need this success."

It was less than two weeks later when my two partners and I launched that company.

What happened next was amazing! We did $100,000 in the next seven days. I couldn't even imagine that much money. My partner sent me two checks for $2,000 each to pay my rent and get me out of the place I was living in. I moved down to Mississippi where we started the long distance company we had been "playing" at for so long, and we made it into a huge success! We did $1.8 million dollars the first year, and then we got an offer to sell out to a company named American Nortel, and we took it in exchange for stock.

Here is a little tip for you, don't take the stock. I have some if you want it. I still have it to this day, but it was a good idea at the time, and that started it all, because I had built a belief system that it could be done. I had seen $1.8 million dollars go through our bank account, and now I knew it was a belief, I believed it was a real possibility. I didn't keep hardly any of that money. In fact, I personally made $40,000 out of the whole deal after we paid our expenses.

What do you think I did with it? I gave away about 75% of that, not to charities or anything like that; people needed things. People would call me and say, "We need this. We need that, etc." I didn't need much, so I gave it away.

During this time, several events happened. My grandmother in the Philippines passed away. My mother called and told me she didn't have the money to get back for the funeral, so I sent her the money for the plane ticket and money to go. To this day, it was the best money I've ever spent. I thank God that I was in a position to be able to do this for my mother. When she arrived in the Philippines she called me and told me that there was no money for the funeral, and they weren't sure what they were going to do. Again, I sent what they needed. This is what money is all about. To be able to do the things you can for your loved ones. It's not about the fancy cars and other material stuff. It's about helping people. The more you realize this, the easier your journey will be.

The rest of it went to support my son and myself a bit. I didn't buy outlandish things. In fact, I had a 1985 Honda Accord and the back window was shot out. It had BB holes. Kids would go by, and they'd shoot BB's at it. I'd only drive it at night, because the cops couldn't see the holes very well. In the light during the day, they could see it more prevalently.

When I was 10 years old, I told my mom, "By the time I'm 25, I'm going to be a millionaire." I didn't hit it when I was 25. I was 26 when I made $1.8 million dollars. *Is that a failure?* No not really. *Did it look like I made a lot of money?* Yes. *Did I?* No. So I didn't really feel I had achieved my goal at that point. But what had I learned from my father? *Never give up!*

INTRODUCTION

"Any intelligent fool can make things bigger and more complex... It takes a touch of genius—and a lot of courage to move in the opposite direction." —Albert Einstein

As I speak with people at seminars all over the world, I am constantly asked, how did you do it? How did you get to where you are today?

- What made me do it differently?

- How did I succeed where others didn't?

- How did I get to be where I am and other people haven't?

- Why is it the people I met five years ago are in the same position now as they were then? That was always a perplexing question.

- How did I do it and other people didn't?

First, let me state that where I am today is merely a minor stop along the way to where I want to be. I'm always looking to improve myself, and my position. I believe when a person stops striving for that next evolution of their life and becomes complacent that's ultimately where they will run into trouble. As human beings we are given so much God-given talent, it is our duty to discover and share it with the world. My journey is far from being over, but let's get back to the point.

As I thought about the questions I get asked, people are wanting to know how I think, how I overcome obstacles, how I get things done more efficiently, how I can analyze a situation and come back with an answer almost instantaneously, that's when I began putting together a format, a system. It wasn't enough for me to come up with some abstract theory which you would need a degree in behavioral human psychology just to understand. Actually, as I mentioned earlier, I don't believe in theories at all. By definition a theory is an UNPROVEN CONCEPT.

I needed something more. I needed a SYSTEM. While many people utilize a lot of individual techniques for productivity and personal growth, most of the time there is no cohesion of the various tactics. Without a flowing cohesion of strategies you have nothing more than the equivalent of band-aids placed about your life.

When done right, a system is designed to be duplicable time and time again no matter who uses it, if the directions are followed. The results should always be the same. This is what I was striving for and ultimately developed with Success Leaves Traces.

Developing Success Leaves Traces and formalizing what I do already, was the most incredible journey for me. I had to sit and break down each individual process, which I took for granted as being natural for me, into steps. This process created a chain reaction of thought which in turn has caused me to greatly improve upon my original vision for it and as result what you'll be discovering within these pages is a much more complete system to understand and follow.

It reminded me of when I was growing up. I was involved in several sports, one of which was practicing Martial Arts. I started when I was 13 years old and rose through the ranks very quickly. It wasn't long until not only was I learning myself, but I was put in charge of a class too. My job was to teach adults and children, who were ranked lower than I was, the proper techniques they needed to learn to achieve their next belt. I had to relearn what I already knew in greater detail in order to train them properly. This meant I not only had to execute the technique perfectly in front of them, but I had to explain why it had to be done in that particular fashion, and break it down step by step in order for them to understand it completely.

Whether it's martial arts, Internet marketing or my success training, what I do is proven not only by myself and my life, but also by the thousands of people whom I've taught methods and strategies to.

What is Success Leaves Traces?

Success Leaves Traces is the five elements that I use each and every time I do anything, some on a grand scale and some on a minute scale, but I go through this five-step process to understand what it is I'm trying to accomplish.

1. Observation
2. Sequence It
3. Amplification
4. Who
5. Timeline

I want to be clear. Success Leaves Traces IS NOT just about money. It can literally be applied to anything you want to achieve in life. Whether it be losing weight, increasing your finances or learning ballroom dancing, if you follow the system, it shouldn't be long until you have achieved your desired goal.

The very essence of Success Leaves Traces is that anything you want to do someone else has already done. If you can retrace the steps they've taken, understand them and even improve upon them, you too can achieve it quicker, faster and more effectively.

In a way, you could say that Success Leaves Traces is a way of re-engineering any task that anyone has ever done, past present and/or future. By using these five key elements, you too can replicate anyone's results, many times over, it can be made even better than the original, if we understand each of the elements.

So, when you're looking at Success Leaves Traces itself, you have to start from the very beginning with the first element. The first step is the most important and you've heard me reference it multiple times already, whether you realize it or not.

Element One

OBSERVATION

"Every man who observes vigilantly and resolves steadfastly grows unconsciously into genius." —Edward G Bulwer-Lytton

Observation is one of the keys to the universe.

Many people tend to ignore that which is obvious. It reminds me of a story I heard a long time ago regarding a legend to the secrets of the universe.

The legend states the gods realized the secrets of the universe were much too powerful for man to understand and comprehend. Even though this power could be used for good, they also knew if this great power fell into the wrong hands the results could be devastating. The gods made a decision. They decided they must hide this knowledge from man forever. The question was, where? Where would this secret be safe from discovery for all eternity? After an endless search of the heavens and earth, they decided to hide the secrets of the universe in the one place where man would never look for it. Where, you ask? They hid it in plain site.

You have to understand, in their infinite wisdom, the gods knew exactly how man would search for these secrets. They knew man would always be in a quest for external fulfillment and would always seek knowledge elsewhere. As I stated, they hid the secret in the last place man would ever look, in their own minds. At least, that's how I heard the story.

What most people do is ignore what is happening all around them. Instead of being in the present, they live in the past or look forward to the future. They ignore the current happenings and opportunities that are going on around them right now. They go on around them completely unnoticed and what should be obvious is kept from them in a mystery—they're so self-centered in their own little universe, they fail to see the world around them.

What I've identified is the fact that successful people tend to observe far greater than the average person. They observe everything. I believe this is what creates the almost mystical power of the ultra successful. When you really start to study the way successful people think, it's almost as if they can foretell the future.

Just think about people about many of the great thinkers and innovators in history. People such as Einstein, Tesla, Edison, Steve Jobs, Bill Gates and many others; they're so in tune with the present, through all the various observations they have made. They could see clearly the subtle changes taking place all around them in real time.

Subtle changes can indicate a current trend or shift in the world. These subtle changes indicate a modification that could mean a certain industry is going to change in one direction or another. These changes can dictate to them what the future may or may not be. You too can learn how to read and recognize these changes and apply this information to your own life.

Observation is the number one element you must learn, especially when trying to accomplish a specific task, whether it's losing weight, building a business, learning how to play a musical instrument, a new hobby or how to play a game, how to drive a car, how to water ski or anything else you want to accomplish. In learning how to do anything; observation is where it all starts.

When I was 15-years old, I was dating this girl, (have you noticed how every story starts with me dating a girl at the time?), and her dad was taking everyone water skiing. He asked if I knew how to water ski and I said, "Absolutely!" Did I really know how to water ski? No, I had no clue, but I had watched a lot of other people water ski. You may be thinking, why would that makes you qualified? It doesn't. But, I had watched, and more importantly *observed* what people did. I watched, and I could see and understand why they did what they did.

Since I was young, I had observed every detail of what a person does when water skiing successfully. One of the things I noticed they did was that they sat down in the water with the tips of their ski's pointing up out of the water. They had their skis up, sitting in the water and waiting for the boat to pull them. One of the things the smart people did was in the grip or how they held the handle. The more advanced people I saw used two hands, one hand over and one hand under on the grip, and they'd hold the stick vertically. I thought those were the smarter people, so I held my stick that way.

I also observed when the boat was getting ready to take off, these people almost always lifted their hands up out of the water to tighten the rope. They knew if there was slack in the rope, it would jerk them, and they wouldn't get up out of the water. I also noticed a couple other things such as, as soon as they got up they always went for the wake, those little waves the boat made and jumped it. It wasn't just sometimes, it was every time, so I just assumed that's what you were supposed to do. Little did I know that was usually only the advanced people who did this.

Like I said, I observed and watched people for years water skiing and decided at that moment, it couldn't be too difficult. Now it was time to put my money where my mouth was. I got down in the water, I had my hands grip the pole the right way, my ski's were pointed up, so I should have a decent take off. My skis were fairly straight and the boat started to go a little bit. I pulled up on the rope; it tightened up. Okay, I'm good. He takes off and boom; I'm up on my feet water skiing. What do I do next? Well, I head for the wake. I leaned and turned a little bit, jumped the wake, and I'm all the way on one side. I come back again and jump over the center. This family thought I had been water skiing for years, so the dad figures he would take me on a little tour.

He took me through the power dam. You have to remember something, when you have a hydro electric power plant, what happens is the power plant pulls in water to spin the turbines, and as a result, it creates these giant whirlpools, like 20'-30' feet around. You don't want to fall in there because it'll suck you underneath into the dam. Now remember, this man thinks I am a pro at skiing, because I looked like one when I didn't have any problems getting up. I was jumping the wake back and forth, I was holding on with one hand, feeling the water with the other hand and doing all kinds of things that would indicate to him that I was a pro.

So what he does next scares me to death. He takes me between all the different whirlpools. As I'm going around, I am almost crapping my pants because I've never water-skied before. The good part of the story is that I didn't fall. I did tell him later on that was my first time skiing, but he didn't believe me and to this day he still doesn't. I did it simply by observation. I started by observing, knowing what to expect and looked at all the obvious signs that were happening.

Let me tell you another story. This is the story of my alter ego, Michael Lee Austin. Michael Lee Austin was strategically engineered in a very specific way. This was my chance to try to make it in the music industry and I did to some degree.

My idea was simple. Create a fictional country music artist and sing under an assumed name and release an album. Sounds insane, doesn't it? It was and it was some of the most fun I've ever had in my life. Here's the story behind the story. The objective was to create a country music artist. From the beginning, I thought if you want to achieve something you have to look at the observations of what success already means. What are the obvious signs of a successful country music artist? I started with the very basics. Years before I ever came up with the idea to become Michael Lee Austin, I was joking around with a friend of mine and we came up with the name. It had always been a dream of mine to do something like this, so we were thinking about what we could name this person.

My friend said "you can't use your real name," but I figured as much, because Armand would be an odd name for a country music artist. It was late one night after we'd had a couple drinks and about 2:00 A.M. we were going back and forth talking about what the name should be. We decided to start with the most common names that everyone is familiar with. We didn't want to introduce anything that was unfamiliar to people, so we jumped on the computer and looked up the most popular names of boys and we came up with Michael.

My friend said I'd have to add something to it, because it can't just be Michael. Remember, I lived in Mississippi for a time. While there, I hung out in Alabama quite a bit and knew some people there. One of the guy's names was Bobby Lee. People didn't call him Bobby, they called him Bobby Lee. Now, it's pretty well known that many people in the south use two names.

I said we could use Michael Lee, plus it has a great reference to the Dukes of Hazard. My initial reference wasn't the military person General Lee, but actually the car from the Dukes of Hazard. We decided that would be perfect and then we started looking at the last name. We wanted to give an idea of being from the south and something that people could easily recognize and not have to think about.

We went through lots of names and then started naming major cities in the south. We tried Dallas and Houston and then came to Austin, which instantly flowed. Then we thought we'd heard of that before, like maybe we knew someone with that name. It had a strange effect because we used all these ideas that were familiar, and together, the name sounded as though we'd heard it before, so it was interesting how we came up with the name.

Once we had the name, we cross-referenced it with all the names of people over the last 50 years of country music history and how many syllables that all the male artists had. We had the name now, so what was the next step? What else can we observe about a country music artist, specifically a male country music artist? I knew a couple different things. First, there was a question, which was hat or no hat because when you looked at a male country music artist typically, you assumed cowboy and hat. Yet, many artists didn't wear hats. So instead of guessing, I did research and discovered that there was a small majority of male country music singers that wore hats. So I decided to wear the hat.

This left the question white or black? For those of you who aren't from the south, the typical rule is from Labor Day to Memorial Day, you wear a dark hat and then during summertime you wear a white hat, Memorial Day to Labor Day. Why? The reason is because in the winter you want the dark hat because if its cold out the dark hat will attract the heat, whereas, in the summer, you want the white hat which will repel the heat. So it wasn't really a matter of white or black hat, except that some people like wearing white hats all the time. For example, George Strait does quite a bit. It was simply a matter of what the time of year was.

The other question, was when you looked at a country music CD, what did you see? You see pictures. Since Success Leaves Traces, if I was going to have my pictures done, do I want just anyone to take my pictures? No. I want someone that has taken pictures for a well-known country music artist before. Think of this phrase 'if it looks like a duck and quacks like a duck, then it must be a duck.' So, I bought a couple of CDs, looked at the front cover and discovered that the same photographer took all the pictures for many of these people. I called him and said, I'm producing an album, and I'd like you to take my pictures.

So the same person who took Garth Brooks' pictures for his album is the person who took the pictures for my album. I needed a cover designed for the CD, so who did I choose? On the inside of every CD cover there was a reference to who created the graphics, so I called that person and told them I was creating a CD and needed them to create the CD cover, that I was having so and so take my pictures and he said he knew him. Therefore, I had him create the CD cover, the same CD graphics guy who does Faith Hill, Tim McGraw and Garth Brooks' CD covers did mine.

Now, I have the black hat, the name, the pictures and the CD covers, so now I need the music. The number one thing was that I needed music that was good, so I found people who had written songs, I had a lot of submissions from people we knew, and I had a certain sound I was going after, so we had the music and then we got the band. The people that played in the band to put the music together were people that have played with big names like George Strait, Gretchen Wilson, Tim McGraw, Faith Hill and Garth Brooks; they'd all played in their bands. This was a compilation of great musicians all put together for this particular artist, so we recorded it down in Nashville. We got everyone together, did the recording and had the music, the song and me singing.

The end result was that we had something that looked like a duck, quacked like a duck and walked like a duck, so it must be a duck. It was all the outside elements, the outside observations that it must be a real country music artist and that's what I used. That's just using the first step of observation.

Now, let's go over this in a little more detail. Success Leaves Traces is a system that will allow you to accomplish anything you want. Look, if it can help me become a best selling Country Music artist, once you learn the system, you'll be able to accomplish anything.

In relation to element number one—observation, whenever we want to accomplish something we simply observe everything there is to know about what we want to achieve. What is it you want to achieve? For example, I want to lose weight. Okay, well what can you observe about a person that has lost weight or a person that is thin. What kinds of exercises do they do? Do they exercise? Are they active? If so, how active? What kinds of foods do they eat? How often do they eat? How much time do they sleep?

Find out everything you possibly can about the objective of what you want to accomplish. Could you eat the way they do? Yes. Do you think they eat more or less than you? Probably more, nine times out of ten, it'll be that they eat more. It's simply what they eat and how often.

It could be because their metabolism is higher, so they can eat more. Also, you may notice their food is a bit different than yours. You may notice they're more active than you, and because they're more active, you can deduce they'll burn more energy and, as a result of burning more energy, increase their metabolism. Everything fits together, doesn't it? You can make deductions by simply observing. Do I need to know that person? No. I can look at multiple people, and I'll find out there are some commonalities.

Let's say I wanted to create a new business. I'd look at people that have created a similar business. What do they have? If it's a physical business, where are they located? Is it a great location? Can you find out what the best location for a business like that is? What kinds of products do they have? What kind of service do they have? What hours are they open?

People start a restaurant, and they really want to succeed in the restaurant business, but they don't know why they're not making enough money. Observe the successful restaurants. If you look around and others are offering lunch and you're only offering dinner, maybe you should do as they do. Should you think about offering breakfast? What kinds of foods are they offering? What kind of food can you offer? Are you offering something competitive? Make a list of all the various observations of what you want to achieve first.

Make a complete list of all the apparent pieces of what you observed about the task that you want to achieve. You have to list every detail. If it was a business color, look, feel; people, how many; cash registers, how many? If it's a clothing store, how many pieces of clothing (tops, bottoms, etc)? What can we observe about it? If it's learning to play the piano, do we need a chair? Do we need a stool? Do we need a piano? Do we need a full piano or not? Can we use an electric keyboard? What do we need? What can we observe about a person that plays the piano?

Many times, the first steps of observation can be accomplished in seconds, but when you're first learning the system of Success Leaves Traces, you need to start there and make it physical by writing it all down. Pick anything you want to achieve and list all the elements of the final result, but don't think about it. I don't want you to think—

just look and write. I want you to see it and write it. Make the list as comprehensive as you possibly can. Take as long as it takes to make it. Just make it as complete as possible.

When you have the list made, then you can take the information and put it in a logical order. That's element number 2—Sequence It.

Element 2

SEQUENCE IT

"Gates is the ultimate programming machine. He believes everything can be defined, examined, reduced to essentials, and rearranged into a logical sequence that will achieve a particular goal." —Stewart Alsop

The second element is to sequence it.

The basic premise of sequencing is taking all of the pieces and deciding what has to be done in what order. You have to decide if something can be done simultaneously and/or chronologically.

Look at your starting point and decide what comes first; what comes second; what comes third and fourth. It has to be in chronological sequence because your mind thinks in a linear way when doing something. What I mean by that is that your mind naturally thinks in terms of a list. Whether you realize it or not, what you are doing is making a list of how to achieve what it is you want to accomplish.

For example, if there was a glass on the table in front of you, and you reached for that glass, your brain tells you, "Move this muscle first, that muscle next and then the next muscle, etc." By the time you're finished, your hand grabs the glass, brings it up to your mouth and then you take a sip. That's how it works.

Our brains work by thinking of what comes first. We're trained and taught to do things in a certain sequence; our brains are even hardwired that way. We know that if the sequence isn't correct, it either won't work or it won't work as effectively.

Let's say you need to go somewhere in your car. It's in your driveway; you click the unlock button on your remote, open the car door and sit down. You put the key in the ignition and start it, press the brake, put it in reverse, let off the brake and press the gas. That's a sequence. While there may be a few minor tweaks to how you do it, it's definitely a sequence.

Now, let's look at what happens when you do things out of order. Sitting in the car cannot be the first action you take. Why? Because the door isn't open. Let's assume you get into the driver's seat. Could you put it in reverse first? No. Because you have to turn the key and start it in order to put it in reverse. Could you put it into reverse first, and then press the brake? No, you can't. Why? Because if we try to put it in reverse first, it's either not going to go, or it's going to shock the car causing it to jump and if you press the brake second, then you're not going anywhere. It has to be done in a certain sequence, or else it just doesn't work.

Life And Success Are All About Sequence

Everything you do in life is through a series of sequences. If done in the right order, tremendous results are achieved. Whereas, if it's completed in the wrong sequence, you don't get the results you anticipated. What most people don't realize is that not only is life a sequence, but success itself is a sequence.

Every major success is attained by a series of smaller successes, and those smaller successes have to be achieved in a certain sequence, or else you won't get the ultimate impact you are looking for. Certainly, not as fast as you'd like. When you are working on any project, it's important to write down your sequence to get the maximum results whether in your personal life or in business.

So, you've made the observations and are sequencing them; you put it in chronological order. Don't think about it being a list; just put it in the proper order. The question you want to ask yourself is, "What's the next logical step?" Just like with the car scenario everything you do can be broken down into logical steps.

Step 1 – Unlock the car

Step 2 – Open the door

Step 3 – Sit in the driver's seat

Step 4 – Put the key in the ignition

Etc.

As you follow the Success Leaves Traces system, you will want to first make your list of observations about whatever it is you want to achieve. Then you want to put that list in sequential order so that you always know what the next logical step is going to be. Don't focus on timing or how long it will take to complete each step in your sequence yet, we'll discuss that later in the book. Just simply put your observations into a logical sequence of steps.

The next question you have to ask is, is there a shortcut?

Create Shortcuts When Possible

Let's say you have a problem on your computer. You're trying like crazy to fix the issue, but you just don't know what's going on. It's freaking out on you, and there isn't anything you know to do in order to fix it. What's the solution? Well, most people would call a friend, spouse, associate or your teenage son/daughter to help. Here's the thing. They look at it and click a few keys, and it's fixed. Why? Because they knew a shortcut—a more efficient way to fix it.

Have you ever noticed that it might take you a certain amount of time to complete a task and then someone else comes along and does the exact same task in half the time? It makes you downright mad, but usually, it's because they know a shortcut. Therefore, you need to take the list of observations after you sequence it and figure out a way to shortcut them.

Combining Steps

First, ask yourself if you really have to do all those steps. Just look at the list. Can any of the steps be done simultaneously? Are they all actual separate steps or can they be combined, putting several steps together? Go through each one and ask yourself what can go together. Can you combine seven and eight together? Can you combine step 25 and 26 together? Could they be done at the same time? That's one way to do it.

Outsource To Shorten The Work You Do

Your second task is to decide if any of the steps are worthy of outsourcing? Can you have other people do any or part of a step? If part of something can be outsourced, it could shorten your time and the work you have to do significantly. You also have to be sure that it is significant enough to outsource it.

Automate The Steps

Thirdly, could you automate any of the steps? Is there software to help or is there a way to automate it so something else can do the work where you don't have to?

The definition of shortcutting, in this particular scenario, is anything that can be done to complete the list faster. Is there anything you can do to complete your list faster?

Remember, this is an exhaustive list. You're not talking about three items; these are all the observations of what it will take for you to get to the goal. This could be a lengthy list of 25, 50, or 100 items. The object is to see how you can accomplish this faster and what shortcuts you can utilize to make that happen.

Remove What's Not Necessary

The fourth question you need to ask yourself is, can you remove anything from the list? Is everything on the list absolutely necessary to reach your goal? Let's say you write down all the things needed to accomplish a task. Step away from it for a period of time and then re-look at it. This could be a few hours or a few days. You may find something there that's just not necessary. Go back and examine it, and use your best judgment to decide if everything on the list is absolutely necessary to get the desired result you want.

Consequences

The question becomes if you remove something, what are the consequences of eliminating it? Remember that every time you remove something from a process, there are consequences. A reaction will happen whether good or bad. Good, meaning it can shorten the process and the time it takes to finish. Bad, meaning something was removed that was vital. If removed and it was a vital component, will it cause more problems in the future for you?

In the short-term you may think, it's not needed now. You may know you'll need it later, but you don't need it now. Well, guess what, if you'll need it later, you have to keep it. If something is removed, if the consequences are too great to overcome, then it's not something you want to do. If it's a vital component and vital to your success, keep it in there!

Believe in What You are Trying to Accomplish

This is key. When you're at the point where you are building this list, you're only at the first step of being able to start the process. You need to believe in what you're doing. You may be creating something, a process, or looking to create a result that has never existed before, and that's okay, but you'll find out that the individual pieces of it may have been accomplished before and that will allow you to build a certain level of belief around it.

Roger Bannister ran the mile in under four minutes on May 6, 1954. Before he accomplished it, doctors all around the world said if a man ran the mile in under four minutes, his heart may burst. Roger proved all of them wrong. At that point in time, no one else had run the mile in under four minutes, but he did it. The interesting fact is that just six weeks later, John Landy broke his record and in the next three years, 16 other people accomplished that once seemingly impossible task. It was because the lid had been blown off of that belief.

Was it a coincidence? No way! It's simply that people's belief became bigger when Roger broke the barrier of proving it could be done. They believed they could do it because someone else had gone before them and done it. When you're trying to do something that someone else has done, you have a level of belief that it can be accomplished. You know they did it, so why can't you?

You have to have the belief and the faith that you can accomplish what it is you want to make happen. As you are doing this, keep in mind the results you want to achieve. You absolutely want to get the best possible results.

My father always told me to never do anything half-a**. I never really asked him what he meant by that, but I assumed it meant not to do anything halfway. I agree with him. *If you're not willing to give it your full 100%, just don't do it at all. You have to do what you're doing with pride and believe that the steps you're taking are a worthwhile progression. Make sure that this is truly what you want to do. If it's not what you really want, stop it, now!*

If you're not willing to give 100% of your effort to completing your goals to the fullest potential, then just don't do it at all. You have to take pride in what you do and believe the task you're performing is a worthwhile while one. You need to make sure that you truly want to do what it is you're doing. If not, then decide early on in the process and change direction. Move your focus to something else, something that you really do believe in.

In life, there are choices. You choose to create the life you live. As you're taking on a particular task, you have to carry it through. Meaning that you have to finish what you start. Many people stop at the observation point and never make a list to sequence. If you've stopped at that point, then you have determined that completing the task wasn't worth it. In fact, you didn't actually want to complete the task at all. I guarantee it. Maybe it looked too difficult or you thought it would take too much time. Whatever the case may be, you decided not to move forward. If it were important enough to you, you would have completed the list. If you didn't, then you didn't want it bad enough. The question I have for you is this, is it worth it?

Build the list first. A list of observations must be accomplished in order to sequence it. Observe everything there is to know about what it is you want to accomplish. How do you know what you want to accomplish if you don't know the end result? Start with the list first, and move on from there.

After You've Made Your List:

1. What can be combined?
2. Can any of the steps be outsourced?
3. Can any of the steps be automated?
4. Can anything be removed from the list?
5. Believe you can accomplish this.

Once the list of observations is compiled and sequenced out, it will be easier to move forward following the Success Leaves Traces system. In the next chapter, we'll discuss how to amplify the sequenced list or how to take your list of observations and make it better.

AMPLIFICATION

"All great masters are chiefly distinguished by the power of adding a second, a third, and perhaps a fourth step in a continuous line. Many a man has taken the first step. With every additional step you enhance immensely the value of your first." — Ralph Waldo Emerson

The next element, in Success Leaves Traces, is amplification. You have your list, you've sequenced it, and now you need to amplify it.

Since the idea of amplification may be new to you, let's define it first. Amplification is a process in which you take an idea and improve upon it in three specific ways; efficiency, time and desired results.

- What can you do to make the task more efficient?

- What can you do to complete the task in less time?

- What can you do to improve upon or increase the desired results?

If your objective was to lose weight, and one of the observations you made was that a person who does physical activity loses weight faster, is there some exercise you could do that would be more efficient, take less time than what most people do and get better results?

If your objective was to put an addition on your house, how could you do it the fastest, best and most efficient way? Well, the obvious option is to have someone more qualified than you to build it. If someone is more qualified, they have more specific knowledge on how to do it, and they can get it done more effectively, in a shorter period of time with better results.

I believe many people make their job harder by believing they are the most qualified person for the task, when in many cases, this is not true. If the task is something which does not require your direct input, my advice to you would be to seriously consider having someone more qualified complete the task.

Each task you have to do in order to accomplish a particular objective must be done in the most efficient manner, shortest time and, if possible, you need to be able to improve upon the end result. If you follow this simple formula, you'll increase the desired outcome and the speed in which your objectives are obtained.

At this point, you need to brainstorm. Look at each one of the observations you've created and deliberate. But there's a key here, and that is you need to brainstorm with the simple idea that nothing is impossible. Too many times, people let their own personal knowledge and opinion get in the way. This is what typically holds them back from achieving true greatness.

They fill their heads with thoughts like, "I can't do that. There's no way I could possibly have that done. There's no way I can do it in that way." In today's day and age, anything is possible. Look for what I refer to as the perfect world scenario.

A perfect world scenario is one in which nothing is impossible. If you had all the resources in the world, how would we accomplish the task?

If nothing was impossible, what would you do in order to accomplish the goal, and how would you do it? Then look to see if it exists, and if it doesn't, can it be created? If it can't be, what's the next best thing? Again, you're looking for a perfect world scenario.

Go at it with an attitude that nothing is impossible or stupid and nothing is out of reach. You want to use a perfect world scenario on each and every one of your observations.

Think Outside Yourself

Forget money. Forget time constraints. Forget knowledge. Forget everything that you know. Think outside yourself.

The problem many people have, is they ONLY think with their own personal knowledge so by default, they inherit their own innate limitations. You don't want to think that way, or you'll never get farther than where you are right now. You want to use the knowledge and the skill that is all around you.

You want to leverage not only your knowledge, but the knowledge of the world as well. People tend to put themselves inside a box. I don't want to sound too cliché about this, but people tend to work inside a very tight and confined space. It's what they're used to and comfortable with, what they know about and that's as far as they go. If anything goes outside of that space, they immediately shut down.

Amplifying Your Observations

When you look at the observations you've made, is there a time-saving way and is there a way to do each and every one of these to get improved upon results and if so, what is it?

Don't just write one idea for each one of your observations. Take each of your observations and make that a project within itself. You want to make a list of as many improvements as you possibly can in as many different ways for each one of those observations. If you do this, you can research and figure out how to make it better. Improve upon it—don't satisfy yourself with what the norm is.

Don't spend too much time on researching or this will ultimately become your crutch as to why you are not completing the actual task at hand.

Improving Upon The Original Idea

When you're trying to create anything, you need to improve upon it. Part of the amplification process is improvement—to make it better than the original idea.

By doing this, you can have something brand new and exciting. You don't want to duplicate it because, as I said earlier, it's not good enough to be as good as everyone else. You want to be better than.

If you want to write a book, think about how everyone else has done it. What can you do differently? Let's look at this book in particular. A typical business book has a lot of great information in it. The strange thing, at least to me, is that many if not most of the greatest non-fiction business books people are raving about actually don't teach you anything specific. They don't show a process. They talk about it, and give you examples, but they never actually showed you or told you WHAT to do.

All you're really doing is expanding your surface knowledge of a particular subject. You're not coming out with a process or a system that you can implement. It's always been a pet peeve of mine, and I did not want to make that same mistake in Success Leaves Traces.

Real estate books are a great example of this. Many of them will talk to you all day long about various techniques, but they don't show you the how-to. Concepts are great, but to me a concept is like a theory. It's not valuable until it's proven work. Personally, I want to know step-by-step. I want to know how to do what was described to me. I want to know how to get to the end result.

You have to ask yourself, why don't more people teach rather than tell? The reason is because there's an accountability factor they have to contend with. If there's an accountability factor attached to it, many will not do it because they don't believe in what they are teaching enough to be held accountable.

Success Leaves Traces is not just a concept. It's a process. It's a system. If you follow each step of the system, when done, you're going to be able to achieve the whole objective—whatever you want to accomplish because it's simple, and it's logical. It's the epitome of success re-engineering.

Success Is Not A Matter of Just Thinking About It

Your positive mental attitude's only part in this process is making you happier about doing it. It doesn't matter how much you think about it because the fact is, you're going to be thinking about it a lot if you go through each step of this process, but you're going to think about it in a practical sense.

Having a positive mental attitude is only part of the process. It will help in making you happier about doing the tasks you are working on, but it will not magically bring you any closer to your ultimate goal. You have to do more than just think about it, and you can't just wish success to happen.

I wish for a lot of things.

It seems the popular thought process in recent years is the Law of Attraction. In essence, you've got to attract success into your life. Honestly, I think it's a bunch of bull. I attract the objectives that I WORK on. I go out and get it. You have to be more proactive than just thinking about it and trying to mentally attract something into your life.

I do believe that if you think about something and you work on it hard enough, it will be attracted into your life due to simple, basic physics. If you work on it, and you're doing it, then you'll have it. That's just the way it is.

With this process, it doesn't matter who you are. You can simply walk through observation. You can simply walk through sequencing it. You can simply walk through amplifying it and then move onto the other steps.

The objective of amplifying is to decide:

1. Can you make it more efficient?
2. Can you do it in a time-saving manner?
3. Can you improve upon your original objective?

Now, you have a list to refer back to, when you come up with the different ways in order to amplify it. You're basically modifying the original task you made earlier in the observation process and amplifying it.

At the end of the amplification process, you should have a new list sitting in front of you. By having that list, you have one primary list of all the observations that you've made, and it's becoming more refined as you go. It's becoming more solidified.

If your objective was originally about exercise, what kind of exercises? You discovered and found out that there are specific exercises that will aid in your weight loss more efficiently than just general exercises.

How about eating better? Maybe you've found certain foods you should eat through the research you've done which have been known to help people lose weight more efficiently or to help maintain weight loss in order to be healthier.

What if your objective is about starting your own business? Let's say you originally thought about marketing physical products through retail outlets but discovered digital products would be much more profitable. Or, instead of marketing to men, your products would be more successful if you marketed to women.

What you're really doing is opening up your mind to many different ideas, but you're also improving upon the process and objective as you go. What is the most efficient way to do it? What is the best way to do it?

Now you should have a list of all the things you've observed. You've created shortcuts and made the list even better. You've removed unnecessary items that shouldn't be part of the whole process and finally, you've amplified it. You now have something totally different from what you started with. It's a new list in chronological order, in a specific sequence, and you've decided that it has to be done a certain way.

This list has morphed into a roadmap, your roadmap to achieving your goals. Now all you have to do is follow the steps in this map and complete each task and soon you will realize your dreams. But before you jump in and just start pounding away on this list, there's another thing you have to think about.

Who's going to do the work?

Element 4

WHO

"The winning team has a dedication. It will have a core of veteran players who set the standards. They will not accept defeat."
— Merlin Olsen

Success is not a solo endeavor. In fact most, if not all the successful people in the world will tell you that they had help along the way. There will be tasks on your list that you are not equipped to do yourself, as well as tasks that you simply will not have time to do. Either way, these tasks can be delegated to others.

Who is going to do it?

So, there's the list that you created. It could be 50 or 100 different items. Of the items on the list, what are you going to do? While you can't necessarily control everyone else, you are the one part that you can control. You control your input. You control your actions. You can improve upon what you do and how you do it.

It's time to go through your list. Decide which items you are going to take responsibility for. On the right hand side of the page, write the word "YOU" next to the items you are personally going to complete yourself.

You're not finished yet. You'll now turn this list into two separate lists. List number one will contain all the items you need to accomplish. List number two will contain all the items that will be completed by others.

Justify Your List

Before you start creating these two new lists, there's one more step to complete…your list needs to be justified. I'm sure your list of items will be much too long. As a matter of fact, you'll probably have yourself listed to take responsibility for most of the items.

Many people, myself included, will automatically put themselves in charge of too many tasks. You'll do it because you're either used to doing things yourself or you feel that no one can do a better or more effective job than you.

That is something I am guilty of also. It's not easy to change, but I'm getting better and am now more comfortable having other people do the tasks. Breaking free of this limiting belief will help you get much more accomplished, if you do it the right way.

Here's how you justify the list of items assigned to you.

From the original list, look at each item that has "you" written after it. Ask yourself…"Am I the best qualified person, in all of the world, to do this?" The answer is either yes or no.

If the answer is yes, put that item on your new "you" list. If the answer is no, the item goes on list number two for others to do.

What you're really doing here is forcing yourself to either admit you're a control freak or make you realize that there is someone else who can do this more effectively than you can.

Keep in mind there will be times where you may not be the most qualified person in the world to do it, but there are circumstances where you have to do it anyway. Circumstances such as lack of money may force you to do it, or parts of it, yourself. Maybe it's personal information or private accounting information that you can't turn over to other people. Don't use this as an out to keep from delegating, just be aware that the situation may arise.

Someone Else

If you're not the one who's best at doing it, the item goes on the second list. The question becomes, "who is best at doing this?" Right now, you may not know.

Let's say you know exactly who the right person for the job is. The first thing I'm going to ask myself is, "Do I know the person?" If the answer is no, the second question becomes, "Who do I know that knows this person?" I'm going to ask all my friends and acquaintances if they know anyone that could make an introduction for me.

If the answer is still no, I may ask if they know anyone who may know them. Here's where the "Six Degrees Of Separation" concept comes in. Eventually I'll find someone who knows someone that can make an introduction for me.

All of this stems from first creating your list. This aspect of creating the list is extremely important so you can make the most out of your time and find the best people to do the tasks you outsource.

Let's use exercise as an example. While you have to do the physical exercise, you may need a personal trainer to help you achieve the results you want. You don't know who it will be, at least not at this point in time, but you know it will be assigned to someone. You may have to research in order to find them. Should the research go on your list of things to do or be assigned to someone else? Justify it with the question, "Am I the best qualified person, in all of the world, to do this?"

Once you determine who is going to do the task, (that you don't do) write their name next to each one of the items on the second list. If you don't know, just leave it blank or write "someone else."

This is important because you need to understand what resources you have going for you at this particular point in time. This is like a collection of all the resources. Meaning, who's going to do it? Am I going to do each one of these tasks? Okay, great. If not, who is?

As you're going through the list, you're thinking, "Okay, Johnny's going to do this and Suzie's going to do that and whoever's going to do this." You may have some idea about who's going to do each one of those items right off the bat. That's great! But in some cases, you're not going to know, and its okay to leave them blank.

Outsource It

Your next objective is to outsource. Outsourcing is something that is not just a single category. It can be broken up into multiple categories.

When I refer to multiple categories, I'm referring to the categories of your life. One category may be financial, another may be business, another may be spiritual and yet another may be your personal life. Don't think of just finances or business. Think of outsourcing the parts of your life that don't require your personal attention.

When most people think of a virtual assistant (VA), they immediately think business, but you can have a personal VA, which means they could do anything you want them to do. They can find you a babysitter. They can make your dinner reservation. They can do the research for you, and leave the final decisions up to you. A virtual assistant can make your life much more efficient. What most people don't know is that many of the common tasks we do on a daily basis can be outsourced.

One of your main objectives might be to get more organized. You can hire a virtual assistant, in some cases, for $6 to $9 an hour. They may be working halfway around the world, but that virtual assistant can do just about anything that you want them to do.

They can look up movie tickets, they can find you a dry cleaner near your house that will pick up and deliver your clothes, they can book your plane tickets, they can really do anything you want. Their physical location is immaterial. They can handle everything for you instead of you having to manage it yourself.

Imagine how your life would be different if you had a virtual assistant in order to help you do the things that you don't need or want to do. When a task comes up, you just forward it onto a virtual assistant and say, "Hey, make an appointment with Harry Jones on Tuesday." They go ahead and make the appointment and put it on your calendar, and you're free to concentrate on items that only you can accomplish. A virtual assistant can give you the peace of mind of knowing that someone is dealing with the more mundane tasks.

This is where a lot of people struggle. I know it's an area that I have to deal with almost every day in my company. Some items are harder to delegate for me than others, even if I'm not the very best person for it. I have to keep reminding myself that it's ridiculous for me to try and do everything myself. I don't have the time and therefore, I need to give it up to my team. In some cases, I leave it up to someone on my team to figure out who's going to do it. The end result is, it gets done in a timely manner without me being involved.

Think about how many aspects of your life can be outsourced. Think how efficient you could operate and how much more you could get accomplished if you had a virtual assistant. You may eventually even need a team of people like I have.

There is a virtual assistant's association on the Internet called IVAA (International Virtual Assistants Association). You should be able to find someone qualified there. You can also Google "virtual assistant." Just be sure you do your due diligence when hiring anyone who will handle your personal information.

Here are a few to look at:

www.AskSunday.com

www.Freelancer.com

www.Guru.com

If you're an iPhone user, ask Siri, which will, based upon your geographic location, give you suggestions based on the questions you ask it. You can ask a question, and it will automatically go through and take care of things for you. You can delegate the work to Siri.

Individual Tasks

Now, let's move to the next stage—Individual Tasks.

You've gone through and marked off what you're going to do and what will be delegated. You've even assigned particular tasks, and there will be some that you won't know who's going to do it until some research is done. Let your VA do the research if that's possible. Just remember that there may be some items that you need to investigate yourself.

For individual tasks, you need what I will call a general contractor. You need a general contractor to come in and do this or that. You're not having them do the entire project, but just a specific task.

Much of the research for finding these individuals can be done online with my favorite Internet tool—Google. Even offline businesses usually have a Web presence. The VA (who is your first or basic outsourcing tool) can help you drill down to find people for this next level of individual task outsourcing.

Don't Let Budget Constraints Stop You

What you're trying to do is find out who is the best person qualified to do the jobs that need outsourcing, and it's usually on a task-specific basis. You may have budget constraints when looking for this type of help, but what if you could work outside your budget?

Think about it. What are some creative ways to finance the best person for this task? Can you get a better person to do the job and figure out a different way to pay them? Is there a way you can trade or barter?

Can you exchange products or services? While everyone is not open to this, it's worth looking into when you have budget constraints. Think outside the box as to how you could you get the best person for that task.

Maintain High Standards, High Quality and High Efficiency

You always want to maintain high standards, high quality and high efficiency. You want to be able to outsource as much as you can and look at different ways to complete your lists and get the job done. This applies to business as well as just about any aspect of your life.

Once the research is done, you should now have your two lists complete. You know what you're going to do and what will be assigned to others as well as who is going to do each task. You can only move on to the next element once this element has been completed. If you have not completed an element, it will not do you one bit of good to move on to the next one.

So, now that you have your list compiled, sequenced, amplified and broken down into two separate lists, you're ready to build your timeline.

Element 5

TIMELINE

"Success is a journey, not a destination." — Ralph Arbitelle

The next element is 'timeline'.

Tasks work better on a timeline. A timeline allows you to not only schedule out the events or tasks that complete an action, but also allows you to clearly see the next step.

This makes it easier to not only finish the task on time, but to stay motivated throughout the process. Now the question is, how long would it take to accomplish each task?

How Long Does It Take

Let's say someone comes up to me and asks a question about doing something. I immediately start thinking of all the steps that it would take to complete that task.

Many times I'll go on a whole rant of how they could do it. "You go to this place, this place and this place." In my head, I'm actually going through each and every step of the Success Leaves Traces process.

I think about all the steps, and as I'm explaining step-by-step to this person, I'm saying you need to get this first, this second, this third, etc. Here's how you would do it, here's how you would have someone else do it, and here's how long it should take.

This is how I think. My goal is to show you how to think in the same way.

It's going to get easier for you too, when you're first starting to think in this linear fashion. It'll be amazing to see how easy you can get any project done. It's also a more efficient way of accomplishing anything.

I'm breaking down how I think so it's more obvious for you. I'm trying to explain it so it can apply to anything you want to do. It applies just as much to riding a bike as it does to building a multi-million dollar business. It applies to losing weight as much as it does to cleaning your computer. It applies to everything you do, so all of this turns into a very simple process.

Now back to your list. The list is actually made up of action items you need to get accomplished, and now you're going to guesstimate how long it's going to take in order to accomplish each specific task.

Many people are smarter than what they let on to be. You already know how long a task is going to take. You may say you don't, but you know. You know there's a process in everything you do in life, so use your best judgment, but always overestimate. Always assume it's going to take longer.

People like to be optimistic. Contractors are notorious for being very optimistic; they're the most optimistic people I know. They're always going to tell you your project will take two weeks, and 60 days later, they're still working on it. If someone says it's going to take five days to accomplish a task, what they really mean is 10 days.

Double What You Think

I think you should double your guesstimate. By doubling your time, it'll always allow room for error. Always leave room for emergencies, holidays or people's birthdays, because you don't know what's going to happen in someone else's life.

Here's an example of what I'm talking about. I had a programmer creating a piece of software for me and the person had to leave because it was his wife's birthday, so he couldn't finish the job. What was I going to say? "No, don't celebrate your wife's birthday." Come on! These things happen, so account for them, build it into your schedule and double the amount of time you expect it to take to complete a task. If you get it done sooner, great, you're ahead of schedule, but always assume it's going to take longer.

Break It Up Into Units

You want to break it up into units. A unit may be days, weeks, months or even years. Let's define this a little more.

If there are 50 items that you need to complete and each item will take you approximately one day, when you double the time, it allows you two days per task. Now you can look at a schedule and figure on average you're going to accomplish three items each week until the project is done. That's your goal and focus.

By breaking the list down into those types of units, three items per week, then you know exactly how long it'll take. If it's three items per week, you know that in roughly 16 weeks you'll complete the project.

Can certain things be done simultaneously? Yes. You can do several items at a time. You say three items each week but there could be six done, just as long as you're always building towards completing the project.

If you don't have a goal and a deadline, tasks never seem to get finished. A classic example is a person trying to lose weight. Maybe they have a high school reunion coming up; therefore, they want to lose weight. That's definitive, isn't it? They have a definitive date they need to lose weight by.

A bride may say I'm getting married; therefore, I need to fit into my dress by a certain date; that's been heard many times. Near summer, people say they need to lose weight to fit into their bathing suit. There are a lot of reasons why people want to lose weight, but it's usually setting a definitive timeframe that makes it work.

Now the question comes up what if it's not finished by that time? What's your backup plan?

Why Doesn't It Matter

Here's a little secret. Most of the time, I don't really want to know why something isn't done because it doesn't matter to me why something isn't done. All I know is that it's not done.

I hear people who ask, "Why is this or that not done?" Who cares? You're basically encouraging and enabling someone to make up an excuse. I really don't care, it doesn't matter and it's not productive in any way shape or form to talk about it. All you know is it's not done. So what do you need to do in order to get it done? That's the question you need to ask, and it's a very important question.

It's the only question that matters at that point. You need to work on the project and have a definitive deadline for when it's to be finished, which gives you something to strive for in order to complete anything you want to do.

This whole process is the fifth element. Does it sound simple in nature? Yes, it does. Is it easy? No, it's simple but not easy. Will it work for almost anything you want? Yes. Is it effective? Absolutely!

Everything Is Possible

Once you start internalizing this to the point that it becomes part of your natural thought process, you'll be amazed at how much you can actually understand in a short period of time, because it's not a matter of if anything is possible anymore; everything is possible. It's a matter of figuring out how to make it possible.

You can throw anything at me, anything, no matter what it is and I will be able to literally repeat back to you the process, the steps and in the correct order of how something needs to be done.

How can I do that?

It's not because I'm smarter than anybody else, it's because I think immediately of how I would do it. I'm breaking down the steps into chronological order, and I'm telling you what would need to be done first, second, third, and so on.

Let's say I wanted to create a guitar manufacturing company, how would I do it?

The first thing I would do is find out what the best possible way is to make a guitar. Second, I would find out who the top guitar manufacturers are in existence right now.

Let's say Martin was the number one company. This is who I would compete against. The first thing I would look at is what are the Martin bodies made out of?

That would be easy enough; I could look up that information, it's public knowledge.

The second thing I would look at is, is there a better type of wood to make a guitar and can I get a better sound if I use a better wood?

Third, I would ask, is there a better process?

Martin uses a specific process, and they produce guitars in mass quantity. Can I figure out a better process or is there a better process already out there that I could use to make my guitars more efficient? Yes.

Is there something that makes the Martin guitars sound better than other guitars? If so, what makes them sound better than other guitars? Then I could ask is there something better that could improve the sound even more?

What are they using for their materials? Are they using oak or some other type of wood? What kinds of inlays are they using on the fret? What are the tuning pegs made of? Are they metal or plastic?

What kind of strings do they normally use? Do they manufacture their own strings or are they using a different type of string? Is that the best string they can use?

I would break down each piece and ask those questions. Who makes it? Do they make it? Is this the best?

Then I would make a list of all the different pieces of my perfect world guitar and find out if there is a way to put this whole guitar together better.

Is there a better way to manufacture it? How would I go about setting up a manufacturing company for guitars? Do I need to set up a manufacturing company for guitars?

Can I find the world's best guitar makers who build by hand and could we team up to use their expertise and knowledge to start this company? By using their expertise, I can get backers by saying I've got the leading experts on guitars working with me, so now let's put some money together and develop this company.

From here, I would make my own guitars and my whole shtick would be I'm not "as good as" Martin, I'm better, and I can prove it!

I've got the best and most knowledgeable people in the world and to increase my credibility, I would get all the famous guitar players I know, and give them free guitars and let them literally say my guitar is better.

I would instantly have a guitar manufacturing company that would produce the highest quality guitars possible, which would be better than the established brand that's over 100 years old.

There's a concept called the leapfrog effect and this is what the Success Leaves Traces concept is built off of. The leapfrog effect basically says you find out what all of your competitors are doing in a specific genre and take the best practices from each of them and put it into whatever it is you want to do.

The example I just used was making guitars. I found out who the number one company was because that's the one everyone wants to beat, so I just started there. I didn't have to go through everyone else unless they had something unique, something better than what Martin is doing.

I would find out the best practice from every company and make a list of all the things that they have.

The next question is how can I make it better or amplify it? Is there a process, something I can do to make this a better product? I would say yes, there are some things that we could do better. Now what I'm going to try and do is put together a product based on what the top products in that industry have and build upon all the new improvements that would make it work more effectively.

Next, I'm going to take that product to the marketplace, with proof that it actually works. What just happened?

I created a better product; I didn't start at the bottom like everyone says you need to do. I started at the top.

Can this same process actually be applied to personal development or something that's not business related?

Let's say I wanted to run a marathon. Has someone run a marathon before? Yes. In fact, millions of people have run marathons before. I don't just want to run a marathon I want to win a marathon. Can I do that? Technically and hypothetically I could, if I wanted to do it bad enough and put the work and training into it.

How would I do that?

First, I would train to run a marathon.

I could go online and find all the famous marathon runners. Are there people teaching a step-by-step system on how to run a marathon? Yes. Here's the question, have any of those people won a marathon? Maybe.

So who do you think I want to listen to, the people who just crossed the finish line or the people that have actually won? The people who have won; I want to know what it took to win that marathon.

What I would be doing is training. Depending on my current physical condition, I may have to ease my body into it. I may have to start off walking.

Set a realistic date and decide that one-year from today I want to run a marathon. What's the objective, what do I need to do? I need to start getting into shape. What kind of shape am I in now? Pretty bad, so I need to get out and start walking. I need to get out there and be able to walk at least one mile before running 26.

I would find out what the marathon experts say I need to do in order to run a marathon and then I would start looking at times. I would start building up my pace. Maybe I'd go from walking one mile to running one mile and walking the second.

Again, whatever the experts recommend is what I'd do. I would start by training to just be able to run 26 miles, but once I was able to do that, I would actually train to win.

You'll find out that there are a lot of experts out there who will teach you what to do and what they did. The thing about runners and most athletes is they track their progress, and they write down their workouts. I could go online and find out the exact workout for many major athletes.

I could find the person that won a specific marathon and find out exactly what they did. Many people are more than happy to tell you. You could even contact them personally and say, "Hey, I noticed you won this particular marathon, what did you do to prepare for it? What was your training workout?"

They may say they ran eight miles on Monday, 10 miles on Tuesday, 15 miles on Wednesday and then they ran eight on Thursday and six on Friday, and on Saturday they'd run a marathon and that was their workout every week.

You need to do the same thing because if you do, maybe you will achieve that same success.

Let's say you followed their schedule for six months, what you're doing is finding where success left traces. You're asking the source and finding out what glimpses are out there. You're simply following the steps to achieve that the same goal. Your next question would be is there a way to make it better?

What did they eat? What is the best thing to eat while running a marathon? Some people who run take gel packs for vitamins, nutrition, etc. Is that the best thing? There are many different variables, but you want to look at how you can improve upon it and do it better than the original person did.

That's part of what you're always trying to do is trying to improve upon it. It's not good enough to be as good as someone else. If there was one principle that I could impress upon you it would be, it's not good enough.

No one remembers number two ever, and when it comes to the concept of Success Leaves Traces; you're doing this to win in life, both personal and business.

You're trying to improve upon the existing successes that people already have. The traces they left behind are merely that—they're traces, simply a small marked pathway.

What you want to do is build a highway through it, because if you can do that it'll make it much easier for you to complete the task in a much faster way.

As a result, where someone else walked; we drive in a luxury sports car. Make sense?

Remember, Success Leaves Traces.

You now know the process I've created and have internalized over the years. The greatest aspect of Success Leaves Traces is that the more you use it, the better you get at it. No one ever comes out of the gate doing it perfect the first time.

As you, yourself implement these strategies, you'll begin to notice changes taking place in the efficiency and the speed at which you accomplish the mundane to the most complex tasks. You'll feel as if nothing is beyond your reach and that's good, because nothing is beyond your grasp.

PRODUCTIVITY

Productivity in the simplest of terms is the ability to get more stuff done. It's how you can get more accomplished in less time.

Before we get too far into actual productivity tools and ideas, I want to share my philosophy on the subject, and why I'm qualified to even talk to you about this.

It's no big secret to the people who know me, that in my company, I have very few people working with me. In fact, I've never had more than nine employees at one time. Most of the time my team has operated with only five to six people on it. Yet, we have accomplished the same amount of work and created the same amount of progress that other companies do with 15, 20, even up to 80 people.

How does a group of five people get as much done as a group of up to 80 people? It's not a new concept by any means, but it's one that is still ignored for the most part—working smarter, not harder.

I believe the average person can do a lot more than what they think they're capable of by working smarter and not harder, but most people think they have to work harder to get it all done.

I mean, everyone knows you will get more done by working harder, right? Not necessarily. Think about a brick wall. Let's say you want to push down that brick wall. You can stand up against it and push all you want; push it as hard as you can, but chances are, it's probably not going to go anywhere no matter how strong you are.

Now let's say I had a bulldozer. If you've got the right tool, that wall would go over with just a small tap. The fact is, it's not about how strong you are or how much or how hard you work. It's about using the right tools in order to get more done.

Leverage is key. It's been said that with a lever big enough you could actually lift the whole world. The fact is, we need to understand how to leverage the tools that we have in order to make these things happen. But we also need to come to the conclusion that we are capable of getting more done without necessarily working longer or harder.

I want to show you the way to get more things accomplished by working LESS. I know that seems contradictory, but the fact is I know that if you follow my lead, you will get more done by working less and it doesn't have to cost you a boatload of money.

It's just a matter of understanding the processes and how it works. Let's go over some basic ideas about how to accomplish more. There are a few different ways to achieve this, but many people are stuck in a certain frame of thought that is limiting what they're doing.

First, we have to look at the limiting factors that are keeping us from getting more done.

Lack of Knowledge: Specifically, specialized knowledge. Maybe you're getting bogged down by Just not knowing how to perform a specific task. There are really only two ways to overcome that: learn it yourself or leverage someone who already knows how to do it.

Man Hours: The usual immediate go to excuse is lack of hours in a day (notice the word I use—excuse) The mainstream thought is that if one person can get X amount done in Y hours, then if I multiply the people that multiplies the amount of hours and therefore the amount that gets done is also multiplied by that much. Right? WRONG! What makes us think this is our belief of how hard we work, and the thought that others work at the same capacity.

That brings us to **Perception**: Whether you work a standard eight-hour day or 20 hours in a day, if you think you are working at 100% capacity, but in actuality are only at 20%, you are limiting your man (or woman) hours. The perception that we need more people to get more done is holding us back because we are telling ourselves that we can't do it all alone. Our limited belief in our own abilities and knowledge can actually be limiting us more than anything else.

Lack of Tools: If you don't have the correct tools to help you, you are naturally less productive. Not having the right tools to keep you organized and track your progress will hold you back. Now that we know what is limiting our productivity, let's look at how we can overcome each one.

Lack of Knowledge: This one is simple. We have to either learn to become proficient in the task at hand or find someone who already knows how to do it and can do it for us.

Outsourcing

I am referring to outsourcing. I am a huge researcher. I look up everything. When I want to know how to do something or learn about a specific topic. I will spend hours researching and going 20, 30 even 50 pages deep in a Google search so I can learn all I can about a subject or task, but researching and learning that stuff can be a big time-suck when you are on a schedule.

I have learned that more often than not, my time is best utilized on the tasks I already know and do well. While I still use my "off" hours (those breaks I give myself throughout the day that have nothing to do with the current task at hand) to learn how to do more things so I can perform them in the future, I still outsource the items I have not yet mastered. Additionally, I know when to have others do the tasks that I really don't like to do.

Let's face it, when we think of all the things that need to be done for a task, there are inevitably portions that we might know how to do but we dread doing them. They could be boring, time consuming, or work you just don't like.

Let me give you an example; I was going through some older videos and realized that they were not up to par visually as my new ones shot on a better camera. My initial thought was, "Crap, I really don't want to edit all these videos one by one." They need to get done but I just simply didn't want to do what it would take to make them right.

All they needed was to be color graded so I outsourced it. I found someone else who could do that task for me, and I let them do it instead of me. While the videos were being corrected by other people, I was able to do other things I needed to get done for that project.

Outsourcing solved three of my limitations in one fell swoop. Knowledge; I hired others who knew how to do it. Man Hours; I had more than one person working on them at a time to get it done faster. Perception; a task I hated doing no longer held me back because I didn't have to do it myself.

Man Hours. The basic premise of outsourcing is to get other qualified people to put in the man hours to do those tasks that you are not able to do or that you do not like doing.

There is a big, big, big misconception about outsourcing. Let me dispel that for you right now! You WILL NOT find one person to do it ALL. Many people set out to outsource and expect to find one person who will fix their website, do their SEO optimization, do all their graphics, social media posting and blogging, answer their emails, fix technical issues and pick up the dry cleaning. Let me tell you….that person doesn't exist! Or if this Superman or Superwoman does exist, trust me, you can't afford them unless you are Bill Gates.

Now don't get me wrong, you will find some outsourcers who can do multiple things. But, typically, when you're outsourcing, you're not going to find one person to do everything that you want. Nor do you want to hire someone who says they can do it all. That person is lying.

Team strategy for outsourcing is the best route. Imagine you're building your own online business. What are the types of tasks you will need to get done? Copywriting for the sales letter, setting up the website, graphics, SEO, customer service, etc.

For each one of those tasks, you want a specialist to do the jobs you can't do. You don't want someone that is okay in a lot of different areas. You want someone who is exceptional in one specific area.

If I get a person who is only 10% proficient at SEO, 10% proficient at copywriting, 10% proficient at websites, and 10% proficient at whatever else, and so on, then they only have 10% of the actual knowledge they need in order to do each task. I want the person that actually knows 100% what they're doing for each project. So, building your unique outsourcing team allows you to get, and pay for, exactly what you need.

I can what you might be thinking now...."But Armand, you don't understand, I don't have the money to hire a whole team!" Outsourcing doesn't require you to keep these people on your payroll long term. You can hire each person on a per project basis. When they are done, they are done. You don't pay them anymore, and that works for each task you outsource. It doesn't take a huge budget to outsource your project tasks.

There are also many different ways to outsource.

Outsourcing is generally thought of as just going to a site and hiring someone, but partnering with another person or bartering with others for services are also ways to successfully outsource without needing any up-front money.

You can partner with another person who has the skills that you are needing. They do one part, you do the other, and you split the money. You can exchange services in order to get something done. If you have a product or service that is desirable, you can offer that as trade for someone doing work for you.

It's a matter of being creative and doing things a little different to take advantage of outsourcing without spending a lot of money. Creativity is a key resource for overcoming one of our other obstacles too!

Change Your Perspective

We can alter our perception of something being unsurmountable by thinking creatively. Quick example–I had been looking to create a recording studio and wanted an ultra modern video wall. My initial research came back, and it showed the project costing somewhere between $10,000 to $15,000. I was having a hard time talking myself into paying that much for what I wanted, and if it was hard to talk myself into it, it was going to be impossible to talk my wife into it!

But I didn't give up. I kept on researching, looking for alternative ways to get it done. The extra research and willingness to be creative in the HOW allowed me to find a solution to get it done for a tenth of the original estimated cost. I was able to think about things a little bit different by changing my perception about how to get what I wanted.

Our perception about money, or the lack thereof, is another huge obstacle. If you want to do something, there's no reason that money should hold you back.

Trust me, I have been there. It's a well-known fact, I started my very first business with less than two dollars in my pocket, and that company went on to do almost two million dollars over the course of the next 10 months.

I HAD to be creative to make it happen. Back in 1995 when I started out, I didn't have a computer. So, what did I do? I went to the library and used theirs. It was that simple. When I needed a fax machine and the library didn't have one, I went to the printing office in town and used theirs. Would it have been easier and faster to have my own computer and fax machine? Sure, but I did what I had to do to compensate and get it done.

Always keep this in mind: *To get to where you want to be, you have to start where you are.* You can moan and groan about not having the tools you want or time you want to do something and get nothing done and go nowhere, or you can change your perspective and realize the tools and resources you have RIGHT NOW are all you need as a starting point to help you grow to what you ultimately want to be.

Tools. Take an assessment of all the different things that you have access to right now and look at them with a different perspective. Chances are, there are lots of things you already have that you can work with in order to make something happen. As you grow, you can upgrade to make life easier.

You always hear that you need "this" to make it happen, or you need "that" to make it happen. We BELIEVE that if we don't have those things already, it will never happen. Our perception allows us to quit before we even begin.

You are told it will take you AT LEAST three weeks to get a good high-end website built. So, guess what happens when you start to work on that site….it takes you three weeks or more to get it finished. I know for a FACT that, with the correct tools, you can get it done in 48 to 36 hours.

Your perception, your belief, has become a self-fulfilling prophecy. If you think it takes you three weeks, then magically, it's takes you three weeks. If you believe it only takes one day or a couple of hours, then it's only going to take one day or a couple of hours in order to get things done. What we need to do is change our perception and what we believe about what is necessary to get what we want.

Remember, Roger Bannister? He changed his perception, and he helped others change many others' perceptions too. While we have to change our perceptions and beliefs, that is not all that is needed. We need the right tools—I don't mean expensive, elaborate gadget. Most of the time, the exact tools we need are easily available to us and are common.

You shouldn't buy tools just for the sake of having tools, though. Growing up, I knew a guy that had every tool you could possibly imagine hanging in his garage. When you needed something thing done, you went to this guy. One day, I was walking in his garage and I noticed that all the tools were clean, but the tool I had come over to borrow was in a junky old tool box under the bench. Those tools on the wall were never used! They were just decoration—to be able to say he had every tool anyone could ever need. If the tool is useless to you, or if a smaller, less expensive tool can work, why buy all the ones you don't need just because it is a cool gizmo.

You want the right tools that will make you more effective. It's time to critically think and assess what it is you really need. I've been like that guy with the tool garage. I have bought things I don't need because they were shiny. I have bought things twice because I forgot I bought it the first time.

Only think about what you really need when you are just starting out—not what you think you want, but what you need. Don't go chasing miracle tools that say they will deliver all the results you want with a magic pill solution. These are usually just myths designed to extract what little cash you may have from you. Get the right tool, when you need it.

Make a List

What is the first step in the process of making any decision? Whether it's changing your mindset or figuring out what tools you need? A list.

I am going to get in trouble with lots of folks for this one, but there is a misunderstanding out there that should be cleared up, and that is a list versus a mind map.

A lot of people will say, "Oh man, don't mess with my mind map. My mind map details all my goals for this project and how to reach them. I love my mind map." Mind maps are fine for what they are, and they do come into play at a certain point in any project, but you need to understand what they really are and how they work. What I refer to as a list is a happy combination of the two.

A mind map is not a productivity tool. It was created as a creativity tool. It's designed for brainstorming, and it is perfect for that. You have a project and start thinking of all the pieces of the puzzle that go into making it come to life. The sub pieces that make up each puzzle piece come out of the brainstorming.

One idea leads to another then another and so forth. We use the map to tie them all together. The brainstorming helps release our creativity and free thinking. I am big believer in free thinking—having no pre-conceptions or pre-judgments about anything.

The mind map lets us write out all that free thinking and organize it and expand it, but that is not a list. It is the broad overview of the project. That broad overview can, in itself, become quite overwhelming.

We want to focus in on the individual sub pieces of each puzzle piece—keep track of each task for that sub piece. A list will keep us productive. A list is not free thinking. It is focused thinking to take what was created in the mind map and make it happen in reality.

I am not referring to just a list of everything that has to happen. I mean an ordered list. Sequencing tasks in specific order of what has to be done first, second, third and so on. This allows us to get things accomplished in a very specific way that keeps one on task and focused to allow the process to get done in the most productive way possible.

Think of our bodies; they naturally work in an ordered sequence. The simple act of picking up a pencil, while it seems unconscious to us, is an ordered sequence of actions that happen.

In order to reach out and pick it up my brain signals my arm to move in a very specific order. It tells my arm to lift at the shoulder, then controls my elbow to straighten or bend to place my hand in the right spot. Then it goes on to control the wrist, fingers and hand muscles.

It may have seemed to happen in a split second and unconsciously, but the reality is, our brain goes through an actual ordered list to pick up something. Our minds and bodies are trained to go through things in sequence and the right sequence. If the sequence isn't followed correctly, or the sequence is not in the correct order, the task cannot be accomplished.

We accomplish most things in life through an ordered sequence. Everyone, from an early age, understands that there is a very specific order to pretty much everything in life. In other words, if we understand that everything works off of a sequence, we can then create the sequence for our task. A sequence can be created by many different factors.

Chronological—the step by step order such as the instructions you get for putting together a piece of furniture. If you don't follow the chronological steps, it won't work.

Complexity—hardest to easiest or vice versa.

The Chronological sequence is self-explanatory and can only be done one way—from beginning to end. It's not like you can start from the last step and move to the first and expect something to work. It must be done in order.

Whereas, complexity sequence could be different for each person. Some start from complex to simple, getting the hardest tasks done and out of the way first and having the tasks get less complex as we get to the end. Others start with the smallest or easiest tasks and "warm up" to move onto the larger, harder tasks.

Starting from easiest to hardest is a natural way to build confidence, especially for those who might be learning something new or just simply have anxiety about projects. By starting with smaller, easier tasks we are building a series of wins each time we complete a task. We get a few things under the belt and we feel like we are on a roll and it gives the confidence to move to something more complex. And by the time we get to what we considered really complex, it doesn't look as daunting, because we have experienced this satisfying series of wins prior.

I prefer to start with the bigger, harder stuff first. I don't need the warm-up——the harder, the better. It lets me immerse myself into the task and wrap my head around the whole project. As I finish each task, the next one is easier than the last and the completion pace gets faster. So, it's like a ball rolling down-hill building momentum.

Both ways are actually correct in order to make things happen and accomplish your goals, but you have to figure out how you work. You see, the key to getting more things done is to understand, on a very honest level, how you work and what makes you work best.

No matter which way you work; complex to easy or small to big, create your ordered sequence of how you will be doing things, and this way you can track your progress.

I want you to remember this phrase—you cannot measure what you don't track.

I practice Taekwondo and actively compete in international tournaments. As part of my training, I watch and study the training of other national teams. In particular, I study the Great Britain Taekwondo team. Every so often their strength and conditioning coach runs the team through a physical test to see exactly where they are. They test jump height, kick strength, running speed, and they chart it all. The chart helps them see if they are progressing. If we're trying to improve or complete something, then you have to be able to measure progress.

It's one thing to say I have this task and it's going to be done, and this is the time frame in which I need to do it in. That's great. You have identified your task and have a time frame for it, but without the ability to measure and track progress you can get so far behind, you won't be able to catch back up.

Whatever goal that you have, whatever process that you want to complete, you need to take that goal and break it down into micro commitments in order to actually achieve it.

Productivity is crucial for success. Getting past your limitations and focusing on the sequenced order of events will put you on the path to success.

CHANGE

"It's never too late to be who you might have been."— George Elliot

When talking about change, I'm referring to it in your personal wellbeing, this includes from a physiological standpoint and from a mental standpoint.

The reason I want to talk about this is because we're all changing all of the time. They say the two things you can count on are death and taxes. In addition to that, you can count on change.

You need to accept it. There is a level of acceptance you must start utilizing. We're going to talk about that level of acceptance, how it applies to various aspects of you and what you should be willing to accept.

I'm referring to the level of success you're willing to accept. This is not a good thing. This is a problem for you whether you know it or not, and here's why. You may be willing to accept $100,000 a year in income. That is what you're willing to accept. That is what your brain is willing to accept. That is what your conscience is willing to accept.

You have at one point in your life set this particular point of acceptance, and decided that this is where you needed to be. Maybe it was through you repeatedly saying, "$100,000 is successful. For me, $100,000 is good enough. If I was making $100,000, I'd be happy."

These are words that you may have spoken into existence by just thinking it, whether you knew it or not. As you have said and used these phrases, throughout your lifetime, they immediately start to manifest themselves into your life.

What happened next? Your income started to rise, and just as fast as it started to rise, BOOM– it stopped. Where did it stop? I will bet that it was near $100,000 because that is what you were willing to accept. Again, acceptance is crucial. That number could've been higher or lower depending on what you have conditioned yourself as willing to accept over the years.

How do you remove that barrier level? Acceptance can be with anything in life; I'm not talking just about money. What about relationships? Your level of acceptance might be to let a person close to you only to a certain degree, but not let them in any further. You're willing to accept that level of closeness.

It might be in dealing with your children, you're willing to accept a certain responsibility with your children. You're willing to accept a certain job; maybe it's your willingness to accept a certain type of car; maybe it's your willingness to accept the way your body is, maybe it's how fit you are.

Again, the level of acceptance is something you need to be conscious and aware of, because, in many cases, this is what is limiting you in what you're doing.

What do you do about this?

- You realize that you have a barrier
- You analyze it
- You discover it
- You acknowledge it

Faith

What do you do, and how do you fix it? There's really only one way to get beyond this level of acceptance where you currently are. The one word that comes to mind when I think about this and how to break away from this level of acceptance is the word faith.

How do you use faith in order to overcome it? First of all, you must realize that in accepting this level of acceptance does exist, you also must realize there is something beyond it. Let's use an example of income. You realize you're at $100,000 in income. I'm just using this as an example, it could also be $50,000, but let's use $100,000 because it sounds much better.

All of a sudden, you realize you're stuck there. You realize this is a problem. You realize the your level of acceptance in your life and in your mind, in the way you act and the things you do is at $100,000, and you cannot move past this point.

What do you do? You have to backtrack. You have to reverse engineer what you're doing to get $100,000. How can you multiply what you're doing that is making you $100,000 in order to get beyond that to the next step, the next phase, the next piece?

Let me be clearer on this. If I know I have five tasks that are primarily producing the majority of my income whether it's five businesses, or five specific tasks that are responsible for my income generation, the question is; can I do more of those same tasks?

Doing more of something doesn't necessarily make it work better. For example, a fly is hitting its head against a window. Doing more of hitting its head against the window is not going to help that fly get through the window. More does not necessarily mean better.

Leverage Your Knowledge

Another thing you need to understand is leverage. When you understand how to leverage the tasks you do in life, you're going to get more accomplished in less time.

How can you leverage what you're doing now to increase or generate bigger and better results? Let's say you own your own business, and you are the only person in your business, how can you leverage it? You can't. There is no other answer—you can't. You could automate it, but again as a one-person business, automation will only get you so far, and you'll cap out again. You're going to have to leverage your knowledge.

How do you leverage your knowledge? You can pass it on to someone else. So now, if you teach one other person what you know, you have twice the amount of work time available.

Just to use an example, I normally have eight working hours. I could go with less sleep or spend less time with my family, but for the most part, I have eight hours to work with. That's reasonable.

If I have one person working for me, I've doubled the amount of work that can be accomplished in eight hours. I still have eight hours, but inside of eight hours, I'm accomplishing 16 hours worth of work.

What if I had two people working for me? Inside of eight hours, I'm getting 24 hours worth of work done. Do you see what I mean? If you had 10 people working for you, you'd be getting 80 hours worth of work out of one eight hour period. That's leverage.

Can you leverage yourself in order to get past that barrier you have in your life and that level of acceptance? Again, the barrier is the level of acceptance. Can you leverage yourself in order to get past it? If you really think about it, I bet in almost every scenario you can.

It could be something as simple as hiring an assistant. You see, whenever you try to leverage yourself, especially in a business, you always think of the cost. "I can't afford it. I can't afford to have that person helping me do this." You need to change your thought process to, "I can't afford NOT to." You can't afford not to have someone else helping you do whatever it may be.

Why? You're not looking at the long-term goal when you think like that. You're thinking of the pettiness of it, meaning the initial cost up front. When you have another person who is working with you, you are getting more done, more accomplished.

You need to train them. You need to duplicate yourself. You need to duplicate the amount of work that's getting done and you need to do this in an effective manner. You need to work with this person in order to expand yourself and the money-making aspects of your life.

Build A Bigger Box

How can you leverage your time to get past this sticking point? The main ingredient to get past this level of acceptance is to simply— take bigger action.

I know it sounds cliché, but when I say bigger action, I mean that you need to expand your boundaries and become more aggressive. People say you need to work outside the box. I'm telling you I want you to be inside the box, but I want you to make the box bigger. If you're going to work inside a box, make it a big box. I want you to do things you've never done before.

Here's why—if you stay where you are, you don't grow, and you don't expand your boundaries. You will never go beyond where you are right now in life, period. There are no ifs, ands, or buts about this. This is it, because where you are right now—that's your current level of thinking. This is your comfort level.

You are inside a box. I would agree with that 100%, but you need to expand the box. You need to make the box bigger. You need to outgrow the box.

How do you do this? You need to take action; you need to get uncomfortable. If doing the things you're doing right now got you where you are, that's great, don't forget them. I'm not going to tell you to stop doing them, but what I am going to ask you is, "What else can you do?"

What is the Next Logical Step?

A question that you should know, understand, and ask yourself is, "What is the next logical step?" I can guarantee you have not done all the steps you can, in any aspect of your life. If you did all the steps, you'd be perfect and you know you're not perfect. I certainly am not perfect; I can guarantee you that one. If you want backup on that, just ask my wife.

So, you need to expand your thinking and take bigger actions. How can we do this, what steps are needed to make this happen? Maybe it's hiring that person that makes you uncomfortable in your business or maybe in a relationship it's saying those words you thought in your mind but couldn't get to come out of your mouth.

Whether you're a man or a woman, it doesn't really matter. People associate a disconnect in a relationship with a man being disconnected from his feelings, not stating them and bringing those up to his spouse or girlfriend, whatever it may be, but women have the same issues and they don't say them. If you want to get closer to somebody, you need to expose more of yourself and your feelings.

The more feelings you express to another person, the closer you can get. Do I do everything like I'm telling you to do? No, but I'm still working on it. I have to work on it as much as you do; the fact is I keep trying. None of us are ever going to be perfect. We're all looking for utopia, but utopia doesn't exist. That's a fact.

It seems kind of strange, but with most things in life, you're trying to be perfect and you just can't, but you're striving to get there. Major religions in the world talk about trying to be a better person—trying to be the perfect person. Can you? In reality you probably can't, but you can try and come very close.

What is the next step? Think about where you are, in what area your level of acceptance actually is. You could have unlimited boundaries in some areas of your life, but have deep levels of acceptance in other aspects of your life. I would dare say of you have a different level of acceptance for the different sides of you—emotional physical, mental and certainly any place in between.

If it's a matter of exercising, it's taking that one step—the next step, and soon enough, you're walking. After that, you walk a little faster and maybe even start jogging a bit.

I heard a great story—I don't know if this is true or not, but it's a great story nonetheless. It's about a man who was fat, I mean very obese. He was sick and tired of it.

He was emotionally depressed and couldn't handle the weight mental or physically. What did he do? He tried to kill himself. How did he try to do it? He ran. He figured he was big enough and heavy enough that if he ran, after a certain period of time, his body couldn't hack it, and he would die of a heart attack. That was his method of trying to get rid of the issue. He tried to kill himself, which I certainly don't suggest, and I'm definitely not a proponent of.

He was very persistent in his efforts, so every day he'd go out and essentially try to run himself to death. As time went on, he noticed that the running got easier. He realized he was making progress and the threat of death went away and the hope of health replaced it. He started realizing he could run, he could walk, he could exercise and it wasn't as bad as he once thought.

Let's think about this. When it comes to fitness in our lives, the biggest problem we all have is not the act of actually doing the physical activity, but it's the pain, which can be the result of the physical activity.

Why do I say this? It's not because of when you do it, you are not physically feeling pain itself—you're not feeling it, but what happens is you have the "day after" affect. The day after you're sore, sometimes so sore you can't move. Sometimes it hurts to even sit down.

That soreness is lingering in the back of your mind and can cause you to want to stop exercising. In life you're either moving towards or moving away from your goals. So, you're either moving towards health or away from health. The fact is you're moving away from pain. The pain everyone feels when exercising makes a lot of people choose not to exercise. Success is the same way. People use varied excuses for not succeeding. Maybe it's because the job is too difficult, or it's a lack of time or money. Whatever is holding you back is just an excuse.

What's Your Reason?

We're all guilty of this in one-way, shape or form. You could probably exercise more than you do and you could probably be in better shape than you are in right now. Why don't we do better? We don't have a big enough reason to do it. That's the bottom line.

What is your reason? Do you have a reason? Is the reason big enough? It sounds pretty simple; "I just need a big enough reason and I'm going to do it." It sounds simplistic, but it's not. I can guarantee you.

Let's use me as an example.

I have a son and a daughter. That's reason enough for me to exercise, wouldn't you think? Logically, yes. Do I? The answer is no. I will come up with an excuse inevitably where I won't do it. What do I do? I convince myself to try to do it my way. Why, because it's not important enough to me yet. You can't succeed for someone else. It has to be personal, it has to be for YOU

You Have To Make A Decision

You need to make the decision. Every day, you make thousands of decisions, every moment of your life, but you need to make a decision as far as what you WANT to do.

Is it a true decision? Meaning, do you really want it? It's either yes or no. There is no in between. "Oh, I kind of do, but…"—then the answer is no. I'm not asking you for anything special. It's either yes or no, one way or the other. There is no in-between. That's what you have to understand.

When it comes to your life, you have to be your best coach, but you also have to be your worst critic. When you're thinking about doing anything, you need to look at it from all angles. Coach yourself on the positives and criticize the negatives to make the decision and the decision has to be final.

This means the decision has to be the one true decision. You can't lie to yourself. You never get anywhere by lying to yourself.

Deep down, when you're in bed at night, getting ready to go to sleep and you're contemplating what happened throughout the day, you're either going to be able to sleep easily and rest peacefully because you know that you did everything in your power to accomplish what you wanted to achieve that day, or you're going to be upset and have regrets as to what you did not achieve that day. It's one or the other.

If you slept peacefully, either:

a) You did try, or b) you've accepted where you are.

Here's where the kink gets thrown in. When someone, like me, shows you that you have a certain level of acceptance that you have adopted into your life.

All of the sudden, (b) no longer exists, because now you recognize your level of acceptance. When you recognize your level of acceptance, you can do one of two things.

Live with it or do something to change it!

Doing That One Thing

Did you ever watch the movie City Slickers? If so, you'll know that in the movie Curly, who is played by Jack Palance said, "The secret to life was this," and he held up one finger. That may be one of the most powerful moments in movie history.

What does it mean?

It's very simple; it's one thing at a time. Do you want to exercise? You're not going to get in shape overnight. If you start today, you're not going to wake up fit tomorrow morning. I'd love for you to have that ability and if you do then tell me how you did it, but that's not what's going to happen. Take it one step at a time.

One step, meaning maybe it's walking for 10 or 15 minutes today. That's a good start. You could start with a one mile at a brisk pace, depending on what kind of shape you're in. Maybe it's something as easy as pushing the plate away when you have reached a certain level of fullness. Maybe that one thing is ordering a different kind of food when you go out to eat.

You see, you can apply this one concept, if you will, to multiple objectives throughout your day. It's the next logical step. Interesting, isn't it? The next logical step is one thing. It's only one thing. Whatever is in front of you is the only thing. Focus on one thing at a time.

The whole concept is simplistic in nature. So simplistic in fact, that most people would glance right over it. It's one of the most easily understood aspects you can do for personal development; one thing—the next logical step. The trick is to know how to be conscious of it.

You're reading this right now, and you're learning about one thing. You're learning this concept, but how do you implement this concept?

Being Obvious

It's called BEING OBVIOUS. To implement one thing or the next logical step into your life, you need to be obvious about it.

Being obvious about it means you need to put a reminder in front of you so you can't forget what goals you're focused on.

Maybe its a little string tied to your finger. Maybe it's buying a ring and putting it on one finger, so you don't forget about your commitment. Maybe it's like the AA program where you carry a little chip around with you. Maybe it's you writing a note to yourself. Maybe it's having a little reminder pop up on your computer.

The point is, keep it in front of you. You're going to forget what you're supposed to do until you're reminded again. Someone can't be with you 24 hours a day, seven days a week, to remind you and say, "Hey, remember that one thing you need to do it right now."

Each and every day, you have all these things around you, in everything that you do. You tend to forget the "one thing," that's the bottom line. You have great intentions, but great intentions lead absolutely nowhere.

When I die I don't want my headstone to read, "He Had Great Intentions." In fact, if anyone puts that on my gravestone, I'm coming back to haunt them. I don't want to be known for having great intentions. I want to be known for taking great action. Do you see the difference?

Having great intentions seems like a cop-out. Taking action is key, but you can't take action on everything at the same time and that's why this one concept, that's why this one thing—the next logical step—makes so much sense.

Think about the different parts of your life. Maybe its fitness, maybe its relationships, maybe its business or maybe it's another aspect of your life you want to do better in. What are your goals? What are your objectives? Let's make a list of four areas of your life.

Don't make a huge list, and you don't need to know EVERYTHING you want to accomplish in these four areas of your life.

Make four columns on a piece of paper, and at the top of each one of those columns write down one of the areas of your life. Under the column title write down the next 10 steps to succeed in that area. Ten simple steps that the next time you are faced with a task in that part of your life, you can remember and do at least one of those 10 steps.

I didn't state how big it needed to be, I didn't state how small it should be either. I said one step. You choose. Don't give yourself an excuse.

Why do I say don't give yourself an excuse? Sometimes what you'll do is you'll have great intentions, but you'll use the excuse that the task is so big that you can't possibly complete it.

So, make it easy for yourself. Do one thing at a time and make it simple. It doesn't matter how big or how small, but you need the 10 steps. That's your task, that's your goal, that's your objective and what you should be doing to bring about real change in your life.

BELIEF

"Though no one can go back and make a brand new start, anyone can start from now and make a brand new ending." — Anonymous

Your level of belief is directly affects your performance and your results. It also affect the people that you interact with. For example, if you were a teacher, the beliefs you have about your students will affect how you treat them, how they respond and ultimately how they perform.

The Pygmallion Effect

If you haven't heard of this before I'm going to spell it out for you. There was a study conducted in 1964, which shows exactly how you need to understand it; it's called the Pygmalion Effect. This psychological phenomenon was first presented by Robert Rosenthal, a professor of psychology at the University of California, Riverside.

The Pygmalion Effect is about how our expectations of other people can create a self-fulfilling prophecy.

The study involved a brand new teacher that was hired to teach a new class of gifted students for the next school year.

What this teacher did not know was that these students had been tested and were found to have very low IQs. Basically, the worst of the worst kids were given to a person who thought and was told that they were gifted children.

Sure enough, when this teacher started teaching, the students began misbehaving. They didn't respond. They didn't learn—but she was convinced and believed that these students were of a higher IQ, so she figured out that they were not the ones with the problem; she was.

After all, they were gifted students and she was a teacher. She should have the ability to teach them. The problem couldn't be with them, it had to be with her.

What happened? The bottom line is she started to take responsibility. She thought maybe her teaching style was too boring; it didn't stimulate them enough or capture their attention. She started to experiment and change the way she taught. She started to encourage them.

She started to arouse their curiosity and challenge them with games and activities and really nurtured these low IQ students.

The more she treated them like gifted students, the more they responded. At the end of the school year, the grades of all the students jumped up tremendously. When they were re-tested, their IQs measured a 20-30 point increase across the board.

She took low IQ students and literally created high IQ students. She did this because of a belief. She believed the students had higher intellects so she treated them as such.

It was her belief. She had built an instant belief system. It was created the moment they told her she was teaching a class of gifted students, because of one thing; trust. She trusted that what she had been told was true. She instantly created the belief that the students she was teaching were gifted.

The fact is, she created an instant belief system based on trust. You see, whenever you're presented with information you can trust 100%, your belief system instantly increases. Your beliefs themselves can even affect your physiology. They can affect you how you feel. They can affect your energy levels.

The Placebo Study

In the 1950's, doctors wanted to investigate if patient's belief in a drug actually made a difference as to whether the drug was effective or not. They would take a drug and test it on a group of people. In one experiment they gave patients sugar pills and then told them that the medicine would be effective in curing the flu, headaches or other things.

To the doctors' surprise, the sugar pills brought almost the exact same level of relief compared to the actual drugs that were used. It was due to the patient's beliefs.

The placebo study showed that beliefs could literally activate the chemicals in a body to bring about a cure. Think about this; beliefs can actually change the chemicals in your body.

Another study was done where they divided 100 medical students into two groups. The first group was given a red pill, and the second group was given a blue pill. The red pill was a stimulant, but they were told it was a depressant. The blue pill was a depressant, but they were told it was a stimulant.

In 50% of the students who took the pills, their bodies reacted the exact same way as if they had taken the actual drug. Meaning, the students who took the red pill reported they felt extremely alert and energetic, despite the fact that they had taken a depressant. Students who took the blue pill reported feeling drowsy even though they had actually taken a stimulant.

How was this possible? Belief and desire combined act as an agent in our cells, tissues and organs, as well as our mind. We can think it to the degree that our bodies will react to the same way we are thinking.

That's why when the FDA approves a drug, it has to go through a double blind placebo test in order to verify its effectiveness. The interesting part is that for the FDA to approve it, the drug only has to perform slightly better than the placebo.

In reality what they're almost saying is that you could take sugar pills and still feel just as good as if you took the actual drugs, if you believed they would work.

Anything Is Possible If You Believe

I want to show you one of the greatest examples of what can happen through belief.

There was a book written not too long ago called *The Psychobiology of Mind Body Healing* by Dr. Earnest Rossi. He wrote about this person named Mr. Wright. Mr. Wright suffered from advanced cancer of the lymph nodes.

He was at such an advanced stage that he developed resistance to every medical treatment that you could possibly imagine. He had huge tumors the size of oranges, on his neck, his groin, his chest and his abdomen. His thoracic duct, or chest, was filled with one to two liters of milky fluid that had to be drawn out every day just so he could breathe.

You have a guy who's dying, bottom line. He was taking oxygen in through a mask just to stay alive. He chose not to give up hope. He was reading magazines, medical digests and anything else he could in order to help himself find a cure for what he had.

He was reading about a new drug that had been discovered, called Crybiozen, which wasn't available yet but was out there. Unfortunately, he didn't qualify for it. In order to qualify for the drug, the patient had to have a life expectancy of at least three to six months. Mr. Wright had been given considerably less time than that.

Mr. Wright started begging, and eventually his doctor decided to go against the rules and give him the drug.

The injections were supposed to be given to him three times a week. He received his first dose on a Friday. When the doctor came back on Monday, he expected to see Mr. Wright in his bed but instead, the doctor found him walking around the hospital and chatting with everybody he could find.

Immediately the doctor thought, "I wonder if all my patients are like this," but none of his other patients reacted the same way. In fact, some of his other patients, were actually worse off than before he gave them the drug. Mr. Wright was the only person who showed brilliant improvement.

When the doctor tested him, he found that the tumors had melted to half their original size within just a few days. The doctor continued giving him the medicine and within 10 days the man who was going to die in less than three months was discharged from the hospital.

He was breathing normally. He was fully active, and it was all because of his belief, but the story doesn't end here. Within two months, reports started coming out on the drug he'd been given that said the drug was ineffective in cancer patients.

When Mr. Wright heard these reports, he started to lose his faith and belief. After two months of practically perfect health, this man relapsed into his original condition and became absolutely miserable. His cancer came back. He had to be re-admitted into the hospital and when the doctor went to investigate, he knew immediately that this was a placebo effect. It was due to Mr. Wright's belief.

What did the doctor do? He lied to his patient and said he heard about a new super refined double strength formula that was to arrive the next day into the hospital. Upon hearing this, Mr. Wright gained back everything he had lost. He was optimistic again and ready for the cure.

The next day, the doctor gave him the injection and he started to feel better again. He gave him the double strength formula, which was nothing but salt water and the tumor melted, the chest fluid vanished, he recovered fully and was discharged for a second time from the hospital.

Two months later, The American Medical Association announced to the press that these tests on Cryobizen were absolutely worthless. They reported that the drug would not cure anything. Within a few days of hearing this, Mr. Wright was readmitted to the hospital and this time his belief was absolutely shattered; his faith was totally gone. In less than two days, he passed away. That's a sad story, but it's also the epitome of belief.

Think about this; a man on his deathbed with cancer believed so strongly he cured himself, except he didn't do it on purpose.

He didn't actually know how to cure himself. The sad part of this whole story was that he had the power to cure himself at any point in time. He already had the level of belief. He experienced it twice. He didn't realize it and no one ever told him. He was not informed or educated in the fact that what he needed was to believe in the power of his own belief.

If he'd just realized that; if someone had just informed him; if he had the knowledge that he could do it himself it may have changed the outcome. I'm not saying you're going to be able to cure yourself of cancer or any other illness, but in this story belief played a large part in both his healing and his death.

I'm not going to let you be like Mr. Wright. I'm going to tell you that you can do absolutely anything you want in life. You can do anything, within any aspect of your life, but you have to have a big enough belief system.

Look at an object. Now, pick it up. Assuming you did what I said, you should be holding the object you were looking at. You saw it, reached out with your hand, put your hand around it, you lifted it up into the air and now you have it in your hand.

That is a success. That is belief. You had a belief that you could pick the object up, your belief was true and you did it. Even simple tasks are governed by your beliefs. If you didn't believe you could pick up the object then you would have had a harder time doing it. The confidence you had allowed you to pick up the object without even thinking about it.

That same type of confidence will allow you to do just about anything you want in life. Your belief will instill the necessary confidence.

Believe Like An Infant

Have you ever just sat and watched an infant? It's quite remarkable, actually.

What's really interesting about children is the way they learn. I absolutely love watching them learn and seeing them figure things out. I like seeing them shocked when they pick up something, and they're surprised they could do it.

I like seeing them startled when a noise is made, and they're trying to figure it out in their brains. You can almost see the gears turning in their heads as something is happening.

Everything they do is building a certain level of belief. All of a sudden their hand somehow makes it up to their mouth and they start to suck on their thumb. The first time a child does it, they got lucky. The second time they do it, they start to get the hang of it. They do it a third time, then a fourth time and all of the sudden they can put their hand up and suck on their thumb at will.

They built a belief system over time. They realized if they moved their arm, moved their muscles in a specific coordinated effort that they would get their thumb in their mouth. They start to have confidence that as long as they keep doing it the same way, they're going to succeed.

It's the same thing with whatever you do in life. It may sound simplistic, and guess what? It is. Once you do anything one time, you have the ability to do it forever. The more you do it, the more success you achieve. Having belief allows you to take bigger and more action throughout the whole process.

Remember Roger Banister and how when he broke the four-minute mile, others did it too? Before he did it, no one believed it could be done. In fact, the coach of the British Olympic team, Harry Andrews, stated this fact. He said, "The mile record of four minutes 12 ¾ seconds will never be broken. It can't be done, it's impossible."

When Roger broke that limited belief, it opened up the doors for others to follow. Is that coincidence? No. It's not coincidence. He not only broke the record, he also broke every other runner in the world's belief system.

When you're thinking about what you're going to do, there's a certain limitation you have. The limitation is the realm of possibility. Your whole life you've been told that certain things are impossible. So much so, that you start to believe it and doubt your own ability.

You need to focus in on your beliefs. You need to focus in on little tasks in order to build yourself up to a point that you are willing to try the big tasks.

Society Is Unfair

Society is unfair in the fact that it only rewards or acknowledges people for the extraordinary accomplishments they have made, and does not recognize the little tasks or accomplishments of the average man. A great example of this is the Boston Marathon. For many years upwards of 40,000 people run 26 grueling miles in the Boston Marathon. How many of those people do we hear about? Only one, the winner. Everyone else goes unnoticed. Yes, this may be an extreme example, but you see my point.

In a perfect world, everyone would be rewarded for not only the big task, but also the little tasks accomplished along the way. If this were done, the odds of success would skyrocket because of the level of encouragement people would receive. Their levels of belief would be tremendous and as a result, their accomplishments would demonstrate it as well.

Each of these stories was based around belief. If you look at any great success story in history, they have one thing in common, that is an extraordinary level of belief in something. That's what you need to build, and that's what you need to have.

Successful people believe in themselves. I have a high level of belief in myself.

The sky is the limit as far as what you can achieve when you have a strong enough belief system. The question is how can you get there? It's not about focusing on the problem of where you are right now, it's about focusing on the solution, so you get where you want to go and believe that you can do anything you want.

STOP FACTOR

"Laugh at yourself, but don't ever aim your doubt at yourself. Be bold. When you embark for strange places, don't leave any of yourself safely on shore. Have the nerve to go into unexplored territory."
— Alan Alda

The Stop Factor is what prevents you from succeeding. Every time you do anything, there are certain signals you receive symbols and signals to stop or to move forward.

As you receive these signals, are you acknowledging the symbols that come with them?

Signals And Symbols

As you go through your life, you're receiving certain signals and seeing certain symbols daily. These signals and symbols are indicates and are meant as guides for you to understand what you should be doing and the direction you should be heading. It's much like a roadmap.

I want you to envision that you're going on a trip from New York City to Los Angeles. When you leave on this trip, you're using a map, which is a good thing, because if you go by the seat of your pants you might get there and then again you might not. Along the way, you receive certain signals, like a traffic light, a signal that tells you what to do. The traffic light will direct you to stop or go forward. You'll also see certain symbols on signs for things like gas stations, food or rest areas as you're passing by.

These indications, whether from a car in front of you or symbols to stop, eat, get gas or whatever it may be, help you in the direction you're going. They help aid you on your way and allow you to know that you're going in the right direction. When you see a sign that says Los Angeles 20 miles ahead, you know you're on the right track.

In your day-to-day life, it's not as plain and simple as that. I wish it were, but it just isn't. It's not as simple as reading a sign or someone telling you you're heading in the right direction because you don't always have that available to you. I know I didn't have that at all, but the advantage you have is that you have someone who has done it before you, they have left the traces for success.

I recognized early on in my career that there were signals, signs and symbols that let me know what I was doing was the right thing to do. Some of the time, I recognized them, but many times, I didn't. Therefore, I made mistakes along the way. So the questions are:

- What are these signs?
- How do I recognize them?

- What forms do they come in?
- How can I understand them?

These signals and symbols aren't always something that you can see in front of you. The first time you receive a signal, it may be something as simple as a feeling. For instance, when getting ready to make a decision, in your gut you will feel a certain way. It could be nausea or maybe queasiness in your stomach, but you never recognized it before as a sign that your about to make a bad decision.

This is your body's way of telling you, "Hey, with everything you know collectively (mind and body), this doesn't feel right and you shouldn't do this." Most people ignore it. People ignore the signs they're receiving from their body. So, what do they do? They make the decision based on what they see with their eyes.

What you see in front of you right now can be very misleading. Your eyes play tricks on you. Imagine standing in the middle of a long, straight railroad track. As you look into the distance, it appears that the two parts of the track actually meet.

It's an optical illusion, of course, but if you relied on that to be the basis of your information to judge whether or not you should go down that track, you would be misled. That's a gross exaggeration, but the fact is, you need to understand and recognize that your eyes will play tricks on you.

Your mind doesn't interpret information the way that it should all the time; we need to look at the symbols.

Nothing More Than Feelings

The first stop factor is feeling. If something does not feel right, you need to stop what you're doing. You should never make a decision if it does not feel right to you.

You need to be aware of your feelings and what they are telling you. So, when you're about to make a decision you need to recognize what your feelings are actually telling you.

Make sure you understand what your feelings are. Keep a notebook handy so you can make a note of your feelings. Every time you make a decision recognize how you feel. Are your hands clammy? Are you starting to sweat? What are you feeling in your stomach? What is happening to you? You should write it down and make note of it.

It's like having heartburn. Most people don't actually know what causes their heartburn. They don't recognize it's the foods they eat that give them heartburn. They need to be aware of what they eat. If they get heartburn, then they need to stop eating that type food.

Once they recognize the foods that give them heartburn, they know not to eat that particular type of food again or to take something prior to eating it.

It's the same when you make a bad decision. What was the feeling? Was it sweaty palms? Were you perspiring heavily? Was it an uneasy feeling in your stomach? Did you get a headache? Did you get a twitch? Our bodies are smarter than we are. We need to recognize these feelings, signs and signals our bodies are giving us internally, and use them to gauge our decisions in everything we do.

The difference between successful and unsuccessful people isn't that they know other people, it's not that they know how someone else is going to react; it's simply a matter of them understanding how they, themselves, react. You need to understand what and who you are, as well as how you react to different information as it's presented to you. This is crucial.

I know when I make a bad decision because there are signs all around me every time I make one. I'm not going to tell you that I never make a bad decision. That would be wrong because I do. I just try to make less of them. The fact is, I recognize the signs a lot more than I used to because I'm aware. I'm aware of what's happening as I make a decision. Many times, I will postpone the decision.

If someone tries to force me to make a decision, they won't like what they hear. When I'm forced to make a decision, the answer is always no. I don't like being bullied and no one should ever be forced into making a decision. I want to understand what I'm getting into—the consequences and what I need to do to make a proper decision, one with which I am comfortable.

Sometimes, I'll wait overnight. The reason why I postpone making the decision is because I want to take into consideration all the factors that are out there. I want to truly understand it.

Consider All The Angles

1. Your Viewpoint—You need to understand it from your point of view when you make that decision.

2. Their Viewpoint—If a person is asking you to make a decision, look at it from their viewpoint.

This is something I've become very adept at is looking at a decision from the other person's viewpoint and it helps me make a better decision, which creates a win-win situation, especially if result of the decision will involve the other person.

3. Third-Party Viewpoint—Meaning, if I walked up to a conversation where two people were talking, and this was the subject, what would an objective viewpoint say? What would be the best move without feelings or emotions being involved? When you look at a decision from a third party point of view, it allows you to step outside yourself.

The reason I say this is because when you are in your personal frame of thinking, you're looking at the benefits for you. That's probably not the best way to make a decision. When you're looking at it from the other person's point of view, you're still biased in many ways because you want to make sure it's a great decision for them, but you always want to make sure it's a good deal for you, as well.

Therefore, you still don't have that unbiased point of view, but when you step outside and look at this from an entirely different angle saying, "Hey, this is someone else's conversation, I'm a mere bystander. If I'm going to give them advice, this is what I would say to them." By looking at it from that point of view and allowing yourself to be in that position, what transpires is that you're now able to give an objective point of view as far as making that decision.

Objectivity

That is so powerful and is key to everything you're doing. When you can look at something objectively and look at it as if you are giving advice to somebody else, your mind says, "This is not you, this is somebody else. If it were somebody else, then this is what I would tell them based upon my own experience."

You've heard the phrase "being too close to the situation to make the right decision." That's how we are every day; we're too close to the decisions we have to make. By putting yourself in a third person point of view, it allows you to make that decision much easier.

It allows you to give a balanced decision, an unbiased decision and a decision that's going to work more logically for you. That's what you need to focus in on and understand when you are looking to make a decision about anything in your business or your life.

When you go shopping for a new car, how do you know it's the right time to buy a new car? It could be just because you feel like getting a new car. It could be because your old car broke down. It's a decision that many people dwell on and wonder if they should actually buy a new car. There are a number of factors to think about when you're looking to buy a new car, but my point in that is that when you make that decision, look at it from a third person point of view.

Buying a new car is a big step, and it's a large investment, so people want to make sure they're making the right decision. What would you tell someone else if they were thinking about buying a new car? What would be your advice to them? When you look at it from that point, it becomes easier to make a wise decision because you can see the answer more clearly.

Use Everyone's Experiences

When you were a child, you made some bad decisions because you didn't have any experience. That's okay. It's part of the learning process. As adults, your decisions shouldn't just be based on your own experiences. Your decisions should be based on your own plus other people's experiences.

You watch the decisions other people make and judge whether it is a good or bad decision. You don't have to rely on your own personal experiences. If you're basing everything you do in life solely on your own personal experience, then you're nothing more than Pavlov's dog. When someone rings a bell, you'll act and that's how you'll always be. There will be no ingenuity. There is no more learning on your part, and you'll only base it on what you've experienced in the past.

That's pretty closed minded, if you ask me. You need to understand other people's experiences and that's one of the reasons I love to read. If I can read information about somebody whether in a book or on the Internet, maybe watching a movie, I can learn things about people and the experiences they've had.

What's interesting about reading and constantly learning new information is that it expands your experience, because now you have added that information to your repertoire. Knowing the mistakes other people or other companies made will allow you to avoid making those same mistakes.

Again, your own experience is certainly a part of it, but when you add other people's experiences through books, audios or movies, you can learn more information, and you're learning for the purpose of experience.

When you really think about it, that's what learning is all about. It's about expanding upon your own experiences so you do not have to make bad decisions.

Let's look at it differently. Not only do you have to judge your experiences and ways of making a decision upon your feelings, experiences and all the other things I've just talked about, but you have to look at the signs around you.

Signs

A sign is being aware of reactions.

Newton said, "Every action has an equal and opposite reaction." I believe that's true. If you push the brake on a car, the car stops; that's the reaction. If you throw a ball at someone, the reaction is hopefully that they catch it. You can also call them consequences, or an equal and opposite reaction.

Life, itself, is like a play. Think of the world as a big stage. If you know the outcome of the play, you can direct your life towards whatever outcome you want.

Have you ever seen a play? Have you ever gone to see the same play more than once? Many people will see the same play a number of times, and they'll interpret it differently each time. They know the outcome of the play already, so they focus on finding things they missed previously.

Sometimes, they've seen the play so many times they could actually tell you what's going to happen next. They could get up on stage and probably direct the actors in what they should be doing.

Many times, you're seeing the play for the first time. You see it but you're not aware of all the little intricacies that are involved in telling the story clearly. You're not living in that moment and what I mean by that is that you need to be aware of everything that's happening everywhere you go.

It's the same in life. You can know the outcome. For example, I know if I do a series of tasks in my business, it's going to make me money. If I repeat those tasks, it will continue to make me more money.

Being Aware

What I'm ultimately saying to you is that you need to be aware of what's happening throughout your life. You need to be living your life consciously aware of what's happening in the different areas of your life.

In business, you know if you have a certain set of sequences you follow, and you follow them in a specific order; you'll get a specific result. If the result is a good one, you do it again. If the result is a bad one and you recognize it, you can avoid doing it in the future. In life, it's the same exact thing. If you did a series of steps and received a bad response, you shouldn't do it again.

Are you aware of what's happening in your life, or are you just being in your life? You need to understand that life is something you live. That sounds weird, but what I'm saying is that you need to be part of it. Life's not a spectator sport. You need to be involved and consciously recognize what is going on.

The reason I say conscious is because you can experience many different things, but at the time you're experiencing them, you don't realize or understand you're experiencing them.

Here's a small test to do to take you one step closer to becoming consciously aware of what's happening to you in your life.

At dinner tonight, when you're sitting down with your family or friends, be aware of the situation. I want you to be consciously aware of what is happening. I want you to be aware of what each person is saying, whether it's a spouse, friend or children.

Stop for a moment, and look at how they eat. Is there a pattern in how they eat? Is there a pattern to the conversation that's taking place at the table? Is there a pattern to what everyone is doing? What are they doing as they're eating?

I also want you to be aware of how you are eating, meaning, I want you to be aware of taking a bite and tasting the food you're eating. How does it taste? How does it smell?

In other words, I want you to experience your own dinner. I want you to be consciously aware of what's happening around you. I want you to literally think to yourself, what's happening right now at this table? What is happening with the food? Where is the food placed? Is the food always placed there? Where is my husband or wife sitting? How are they eating? Do they talk with food in their mouths? Where are the children sitting? Do they always sit in the same place? What is the conversation like?

The purpose of this task is to bring you into your own life and not just be a spectator in it. I want you to consciously be aware of what's happening to you for the 30 minutes to an hour or however, long it takes, for you to eat dinner.

Little tasks like this allow you to experience life. Be aware of what's happening to you at that time. Some people call it living in the moment, but I want you to understand and appreciate all the things that are happening around you. Be consciously aware of reactions. Be consciously aware of body movements. Be consciously aware of facial expressions.

The purpose of the exercise is to allow you to be involved, not only to live your life, but also to be aware of it and actually experience it.

If you have an argument with your spouse or significant other, be consciously aware of what you're doing and how they react; understand and listen to what they're saying.

Do this more and more. If you're in business, be consciously aware of what is happening when you're in talks or negotiations. Be consciously aware of what is happening in your business.

It will make you more productive. It will allow you to make better decisions and, it will allow you to consciously retain more information.

Subconsciously, you're recording everything happening around you right now. You are only a piece of the puzzle—one part. There are other parts and you need to be aware of what they are and what they are doing.

A while back, I made a decision to hold a seminar called Freedom Factor. As soon as I made that decision there were signs all around me. I had three or four promoters contact me, and they didn't want me to talk about Internet marketing, they wanted me to talk about success.

The signs were easily recognizable. One day after the decision was made, people were contacting and asking me to speak on success. I understood that. I understood what was happening, I was aware of what was happening. This was a sign, a symbol, letting me know that I made the correct decision.

This is what you need to look out for. When you make a decision, are there signs letting you know you made the right choice?

For many years, I knew this was a direction that I would be heading into. I knew it, because it rested well within me. That decision has been further validated, because this book is a direct result of that event.

Trust Yourself

I want to ask you a question. Are you doing what you should be doing right now with your life? When you read that, you immediately got an answer, and it was the right answer. It was either yes or no. You see, when you are asked a direct question your subconscious will answer it. More often than not, people will disregard the immediate answer and try to rationalize what the answer should be.

Listen to your gut and recognize what answers you are receiving. Now, the question is, if you're not doing what you should be doing, what should you be doing? Did you get your answer?

You may have been putting it off or trying to get away from it, but the fact is you know what you should be doing right now. The question is, why aren't you doing it?

I believe we are all here for a purpose. I believe everyone has a calling in life. Once you start doing what you should be doing, everything else falls into place for you. The signs will come unbelievably fast, so be ready.

Trust the signs. Trust yourself. You already know the answers. You know what you need to do. You just need to trust yourself more.

If you feel that you are not doing what you should be doing in life, then you need to start doing what you should be doing. I'm not saying you should give up what you're currently doing, quit your job and move to Africa or China; it doesn't have to be that drastic. Just start moving in the right direction, even if you start with baby steps; starting is the hardest step.

As you already know, I sold vacuum cleaners for over five years, but I'll always remember the first day I was told to go out and knock on doors by myself. The hardest door for me to get through was the door of my car, the one right next to me.

Once I got out of my car, it really wasn't that hard. You need to understand that the first step is the hardest. I understand it's hard to do, and I can appreciate the apprehension felt when you attempt to do something new.

You need to understand that it's okay if it's not easy at first. It's okay that you're not good at it at first. Greatness doesn't always come easy. Genius doesn't always come easy. What you do in life is not necessarily going to be easy for you.

I'm passionate about music. I love being Michael Lee Austin. When I first started, it was difficult and still is to this very day.

I know I'm not the greatest singer in the world. I know I don't have the most talent, and that's okay. Can I sing? Yes. I feel that I am as good or better then a lot of people out there, but I had to continuously work on it day in and day out.

If you heard the recordings of what I sounded like when I first started versus what I sound like today, there's been a complete transformation for the better. I'm still not going to be the greatest singer in the world, but did I make a drastic improvement? You bet! Was it easy? No.

You need to understand that it's not going to be easy. You may be a natural or you may not. Don't worry about it. It doesn't matter. The fact is, as long as you start doing it, the signs will start appearing. The symbols will be there, and reactions from other people will be there and the right people will be drawn to you.

In many cases, as the right people are drawn to you, oddly enough, they are usually preceded by the wrong people. That's where living in the moment, being conscious and aware of the people you're dealing with allows you to make the right decisions.

Some of the people I was working with in my recording business seemed to be great people. They said all the right things, treated me great and had all the right contacts, but something wasn't right. I told one of my business partners that they were great guys, but there was something about one of them that I just didn't like. I couldn't put my finger on it, it was just a feeling I had. The interesting part was that my business partner had the same feeling. Ultimately, we stopped doing business with them.

The reason I bring up this particular situation is because it was overwhelming; it wasn't a small feeling—it was huge. I met them and from that moment I had a bad feeling.

It was so overwhelming to me that it literally jumped off the page and stopped me from doing any business with them. If you have a feeling that strong, it shouldn't be ignored.

You need to be aware of those types of feelings when you meet people.

You need to be conscious of who you are what you feel inside when you're making decisions when talking to someone. What's happening to your body. Becoming conscious of that is step one. Step two is being aware of your surroundings and understanding the signs and symbols around you right now.

Knowing The Limitations

As you're going through this whole process, you need to be fully aware of limitations when dealing with other people.

Is there a limitation in dealing with a person? Is there something you don't like? What is it you don't like? It doesn't have to be logical, but remember, it's all part of the processes you go through in your daily life.

What's your objective for today? It's to be conscious during dinner. I'm talking about you being conscious of your environment, what everyone else is doing and what you're doing while you're eating dinner. That's what I want you to focus in on. This will allow you to notice how you consciously are aware of what's going on in your surroundings.

Be conscious of what you're doing throughout the day and periodically ask yourself what you're doing. When you're in a meeting with others, ask yourself, "What's happening?" Asking questions will allow you to be consciously aware of what's going on in your environment.

Your reactions are something you've been trained to have. You'd like to think that your instincts are well trained, but that's not true. Your instincts are based upon what you've experienced. You need to stop and look at the situation for what it is. Put yourself in the third party standpoint and look at it from a totally objective point of view. Give yourself advice; you're now in control.

If you do all the things discussed in this chapter and allow yourself to become completely aware of what's going on around you, it will help you make better decisions. It will help you in every aspect of your life. I can't be there to hold your hand and say, "Do this or do that." You have to do it for yourself.

Stop going through the motions and start actively living your life. There are all kinds of stop factors out there. They're everywhere, and if you're not aware of the signs and symbols that are naturally guiding you to make the right decisions, then those stop factors could keep you from achieving your full potential.

Read the signs, follow the symbols, trust yourself and succeed.

SUPER SELF

"Our deepest fear is not that we are inadequate. Our deepest fear is that we are powerful beyond measure." —Marianne Williamson

My Super Self took me from a successful businessman to an innovator and Internet trendsetter, a best selling country western singer and an international speaker, allowing me to use a certain mindset and several powerful tools on my journey to success. They include:

- Training Your Mind
- Super Self = Achieving Your Goals
- Subconscious to Conscious
- Building Your Super Self

Training Your Mind

Every athlete knows to properly train your body you must first train your mind. Success comes to those who have the willpower and the strength to persevere when times get tough. Even through physical challenges, most of the battle of finishing the race and making it to the top takes place in your mind. When the mind is strong, it will keep your body moving forward until you reach your goal.

It is for that reason that with the Success Leaves Traces system, my focus is to take you outside of your element and instill a sense of confidence and the desire to push yourself farther than you have ever gone before. Follow the traces of success left behind by those who have gone before you and you create your most powerful you, what I call your Super Self.

There are a couple of important points that will help you understand the concept of Super Self and the mindset necessary to create it.

Success Leaves Traces focuses on bringing awareness that the trail has already been blazed for you. There are so many people throughout history, who have become successful with a Super Self mindset, and you can follow in their footsteps. Along with rethinking and refocusing, you can become successful much faster.

You Have The Answers Within

You already have the answers inside of you. You ask yourself thousands of questions every single day. It sometimes seems that the harder you try to make a change, the more resistance you encounter.

Whether you realize it or not, you already have the answers to all of your questions. You have been exposed to so many things in your life, and you do not realize exactly how much knowledge you already have obtained. You have the tools within you to overcome obstacles. You forget almost all the information you have learned, and you only process 2-3% of what is happening at any given point in your life.

Although there are literally millions of events going on around you all the time, your mind is only processing about 40 items at a time.

Just take a look around. What's going on? If you're near a window, perhaps you can see nature carrying on outside, maybe you can hear an air conditioner running or the sound of shuffling papers.

If the television is on, you are most likely being bombarded by many different scenes. As all these things are going on around you, your mind is absorbing and remembering, whether you realize it or not. How much information are you missing? How much have you tuned out or thought to be insignificant?

When someone speaks, in addition to hearing what they are saying, you are also processing their meaning, their body language, the way they look, the way their hair is combed, the tone of voice, their eye movements, mouth movements and gestures they make with their hands. Your brain is processing all kinds of information you are not aware of at the time it is taking place.

Each day you interact, process, remember, retain, and discard. It's a process you do over and over again, day after day and it's mostly all done in your subconscious mind.

Can you imagine how much information has been processed throughout your entire life? Whether you learned it from a book, saw it in a movie, or heard it from a friend, you actually have all that information stored within you. The challenge is accessing it.

Limiting Success Filters

Why does your mind suppress this information?

When you have a task to do, your brain only accesses the information it feels you can handle at that particular time. Why? What is that filter that gets put into place? There are several filters that your brain uses. I call them "Limiting Success Filters" because by limiting the amount of information your brain can access at one time, it in turn, limits your potential for success.

One of the primary focuses of these filters is based upon your self-esteem or how you view yourself as a person and your potential to succeed in life. You subconsciously place your own filter into your brain functions. It's placed there based on the way you act, the way you perform, and the way you do things. You may not realize it, but your level of self-esteem, if low, may be what's been holding you back from success your entire life.

You may actually be your own worst enemy if you don't feel worthy of having something really great in your life. You may be self-sabotaging any chance at success you've ever had and not even realize what you're doing.

Success Catalysts

There are techniques that can be used to cause your subconscious to release some of the information. These are what I call "Success Catalysts." You can actually bring up bits of information at any given point in time. There are specific techniques in bringing the information you've stored from your subconscious to your conscious.

You need a "Whatever It Takes" Attitude. The phrase itself means no matter what. You will achieve your goal without any conditions. "No matter what it takes, I will get the job done. I will complete the task. I will achieve the goal." This is a winning attitude.

Many times conditioning and environment plays a part in someone having low self esteem. The conditioning you experienced throughout your life, up until today, is not your fault. Perhaps until this moment you were not aware that your environment could affect your ability to succeed. Not being aware could very well affect and limit your success. This took me a long time to understand, but once I understood it, it made a big difference in my life.

Most children do not get success training. Even though your parents may have done a great job in raising you, they may not have taught you the success lessons that would allow you to become successful. They may have taught you strategies on how to get by in life, and those strategies were based on what they had learned.

I was raised by parents who taught me right from wrong and how to be respectful of others. They taught me many things I am grateful for, and they were great parents. I have a lot of fantastic memories from my childhood.

My parents taught me lessons that they thought I could use in life to make me a productive and independent person, but my parents had not become successful in the financial world. They were not living their dream, so they were only able to teach me what they knew.

Neither of my parents were able to teach me about financial success. Even as a child growing up, I knew that I was not learning lessons of success because we did not live in a big, fancy house. I am not saying success is all about material things, but as a child, I knew instinctively that there was more to learn about life than what I was learning at home. As I grew older and started yearning for and desiring success, I had to replace my old beliefs about achieving success with a different way of thinking before I could succeed in my ventures.

Super Self = Achieving Your Goals

You have to be responsible for your own life and success. No matter what your upbringing was, from this point forward, if you fail to achieve your goals, the failure can only be blamed on you. You are responsible for your current environment. You have to take responsibility for where you are in life right now. Until you do, you will have a need or will want to place the blame on somebody else for your lack of whatever it is that you desire in life.

One big lesson my mom taught me was that you can do anything you want, if you want it bad enough. "You can have anything you want, if you want it bad enough." She told me that over and over.

My mom was a tiny, little Filipino woman, not even five feet tall, yet her words of encouragement got me through many challenges as I struggled to make my own way in the world. If you are willing to put forth the effort, then yes, you CAN achieve success. If you are not willing to work hard, then it is not going to happen for you. It's a simple fact! Those simple words that my mom told me made a huge difference on my outlook on life.

Take Responsibility

To create a Super Self, you must take responsibility. You have to take control of your life, your thoughts and your environment. Your thoughts and environment are very closely related. By changing your environment, you can certainly change your thoughts.

It all depends on your circumstances and how you perceive reality. You can create change instantly if you want to. It all comes down to your comfort level. The more uncomfortable you are, the more you are willing to work, the more change you can create. The fact is that many of us are too comfortable where we are right now.

What is your driving force? There are only two things that will determine your success or ability to accomplish a specific goal—pain or reward.

You tend to do something because either the pain is so great that you have to do it in order to make the pain go away, or the desire or the reward is so great that you must do it. You are either moving away from something or moving toward something. Everything that you do in life is based around these two things. It is either one or the other. The pain is the driving force; the desire or the reward is the driving force. You have to recognize your driving force and use it. Can the two exist at the same time? Yes — 100% — yes!

Subconscious to Conscious

Awareness is key to everything you do in life. It is needed for self-realization. Before you can move forward with change, you must first be aware of your current position. This is your starting point.

You now need to formulate a plan and a path. The fact is that this is who you are. You cannot expect in whole that you can change your thinking quickly based upon your circumstances and your environment. Your environment allows you to change your thinking very quickly, but you can't expect a long-lasting change to take place immediately. You can change your environment right away and work hard enough and change your thinking long enough to get back to your natural environment, but for long-term effects to take place, you first need to formulate a plan and a path.

It's time to delegate tasks in areas where you are weak. Know your own strengths and weaknesses, and make the best of your strengths. For example, I am very poor at following up with people. After realizing the problem, I had to create a solution to remedy it. The solution was to build my team with people who had great follow up skills. I surround myself with people who are great at what I am worst at, and this produces great results. My strengths grow stronger and my weaknesses are still there but are not highlighted.

You must become aware of who you are, and play on your strengths and diminish your weaknesses. You are not going to do that overnight, but you need to focus in on how you are going to accomplish this objective of becoming successful. Become aware of who you are so that you can move forward.

I recommend you use a success journal in order to make this happen. Your success journal will begin with who you are right now. What are your strengths, and what are your weaknesses?

Let's start your success journal right now. There is no reason to procrastinate. Get a notebook or even a sheet of paper. Let's start off with a list of your strengths.

Write them all down. Include strengths in an area in your life that you're currently focused on improving or all of the areas in your life that need improvement. Include personal, financial, spiritual, professional, and any other area where you need to focus on right now.

You may have to dig deep to come up with an accurate list of your strengths. Take time and go over details of everything you do. What have others said about you? Is there anything you're complimented on regularly? Have you accomplished something specific in an area of your life? If you are struggling with this list, call a good friend or family member, someone who will tell you the brutal truth, no matter what. That person will be able to help pinpoint your strengths and possibly any weaknesses you may not be aware of.

Now, think about your weaknesses. What is it that is affecting you? What are the problems you currently have? Those are your weaknesses. Again, include weaknesses in each area of your life, or in just the area in which you are focusing. Be honest with yourself in this list.

You may be wondering what is the real purpose of this? Why do you need to be so honest with yourself about your strengths and weaknesses? I want to build you up and get you on your way to success. You are creating a self-assessment so that you can become aware of the person you currently are. You want to build on who you are to create your Super Self, but you must first discover who "you" really is. By doing this, you are getting to know your starting point. This starting point has been set by your past and present environment, thought processes, and mindset, but your finishing point is something you've yet to create.

You don't have to base where you finish on where you start. No matter how much work you have to do internally and externally, how much growing up you have to do, how much maturing you have to do, or how much learning you have to do, if you're willing to put forth the effort to make of yourself what you want to be, you can reach any goal you have in life. So, don't let your starting point frustrate you. If you have a laundry list of weaknesses and only a handful of strengths, don't let that stop or intimidate you. I have many weaknesses that I've had to acknowledge and overcome. You're human and not perfect. There isn't a person alive who is good at everything they do, no matter how much they like to think they are, so don't get caught up in the list. Focus on what you can do to work with who you are right now.

Determining strengths and weaknesses is the entry point in the road to success. You now have your lists. You have acknowledged your strengths and weaknesses and know what you need to work on in your life. The strengths are the things you need to work with to make yourself even stronger.

Until you have done this, you have not yet begun to travel the road to success. You have not yet begun to follow the traces to success. I'm leaving a trace now for you to follow. Whether you pick up your pen or your pencil and make your lists by facing your true self and discovering where you are in life right now is up to you.

Choose to follow in my footsteps. It's like the old saying, "You can lead a horse to water, but you can't make him drink." This entire concept of Success Leaves Traces is built on your following in the footsteps of those who have already walked the pathway to success. I can give you the knowledge to find the pathway that you should follow. I can provide you with the tools to work with who you are to better yourself and to be able to find success, but I can't force you to use anything that I've taught you in the pages of this book. I can't force you to step on that path. You have to do it for yourself.

Until you're ready to make the commitment it takes to utilize these methods and break out of your box, you won't reach your long-term goals. It's as simple as that. If you skipped the step of listing your strengths and weaknesses and discovering who you are and where you are right now, then you've not made a commitment to make a change.

You deserve to have better in life! You deserve to live your dream! Create your starting point and move on to the next step. You are now ready to create your Super Self and start making fast tracks to your success.

Building Your Super Self

Your Super Self is an enhanced and perfect version of yourself. Imagine someone just like you. They look like you, walk like you, talk like you—with one additional feature—they are perfect. They have all the answers, and they know all the questions. They know everything; they are Google and Wikipedia rolled into one. It's time to create your Super Self.

Below is what I want you to do to get in touch with your Super Self—your new superhero and an infinite resource.

- Pick a quiet spot, get centered, close your eyes.
- Mentally look in front of you.

- Imagine your Super Self sitting across from you. They are your Super Self twin—they look, walk, talk, sound just like you.

- Know that your Super Self has all the answers—to whatever questions you may have. Your Super Self remembers everything you have learned and everything you have forgotten you learned.

- You are going to ask your Super Self questions and Super Self is going to give you the correct answers because Super Self knows everything you have observed your whole life.

- Each time you ask questions, view yourself giving the right answers.

You may be thinking, "What is he talking about? This is ridiculous." Have faith and keep reading. This is the same technique Napoleon Hill used in his trainings and his mastermind principle—it works! Now, imagine yourself asking the question, "If you wanted to be a better person, where would you start?"

You can say this in your head or out loud to Super Self. By asking a question, listening, and expecting an answer, you will get an answer. Your Super Self is actually recalling back into memory everything that you have learned and coming back with the answer. Your Super Self remembers everything you ever said, were supposed to remember, read, saw, heard and learned. Super Self remembers all these different things and has the answer. You have to expect the answer.

If you do not understand the answer, simply say, "Explain that a little more. What did you mean by that?" and wait for the answer. By visualizing that you are talking to another person, it commands your brain to research the questions and deliver the answers. Your brain knows because you asked a question, you expect an answer. Your brain will ultimately dig down into the depths of your subconscious, into the depths of your memory, to go deeper than it has ever gone before to give you the correct answer.

This entire process can take place in seconds. The more you practice this technique, the better and faster it will become. This process also has an additional benefit. As you are asking questions, you are visualizing yourself giving the correct answer back to you. Doing this is actually building your self-esteem. You are now viewing yourself as the person with all the answers. You are viewing yourself to be intelligent, to be all knowing. You are viewing yourself as the person you should be. This raises your self-confidence in a big way. By repeating this process over and over again, you get more self-assured, and you learn to trust yourself.

When you take responsibility for who you are, when you know your strengths and weaknesses, when you start seeing yourself as the perfect person, essentially the person that you want to be, when you begin to see and trust your Super Self on a consistent basis, you start building other parts of your inner self. You start being the person that you want to be.

Trust Your Super Self

Trust is an important factor here; it is an essential element. You have to trust that you do have the answers. I know that you have the answers to any question you could possibly ever ask yourself. This technique will give you total access to all the answers. By using this technique, and learning to trust yourself, you are gaining access to a whole new world that you have not yet discovered. This is the change—the turning point. This is how you achieve overwhelming success: you accept that you can move through any challenges, go forward and create the desire, avoid the pain and build your life the way you envision it. As you use these techniques more and more, you will access a different level of yourself, a level that very few people reach. That is the edge that will make a massive difference to your success.

Trust leads to experience, which leads to results, which leads to success. The more success you achieve, the more trustworthy your beliefs. The more you believe and trust in Super Self, the more you will ultimately learn to trust yourself—which keeps the cycle to success moving forward.

Everyone makes daily decisions. Whether it is to ride a bicycle, get married or move to another town, no matter what it is, you will make many decisions in your lifetime. Keep in mind that hopes, wishes, and dreams are not decisions. In your heart, when you made that decision, you knew that you would not be able to accomplish whatever it was. This is not what I refer to as a true decision.

True Decisions

The true decision is the toughest type of decision to make, and it is also the most rewarding. It's the decision that you ultimately really want. It means that once you make the decision to do something, you will do whatever it takes to achieve your goal. A true decision is unconditional. A true decision can determine success. You may not have made a change in your life because you have not made the true decision that you truly want your dreams and your goals.

What you have to realize to achieve them, it starts off with the true decision. A true decision is not something you make hastily; it takes time and should be well thought out. A true decision must also be the right decision for you and your family. This is not a wish. This is not a dream. This is not, "I hope for that." This is, "I am going to!"

Once you have made the decision, every part of your being, including your thinking process and your emotions becomes aligned with it. That decision will guide you and your life. All of a sudden, magic happens. That may sound strange, but I am telling you once you make that true decision, it will put you on the right path and it will be obvious to you. I believe that once you are on the right path, you are in tune with what you are supposed to be doing with your life; things happen, opportunities appear and doors begin to open for you. That true decision is crucial to your success.

I know it sounds cliché, but you have the power within you. You have the capability to achieve your dreams and transform your life into the lifestyle you have always wanted. The Super Self is part of it. It comes down, ultimately, to the realization that you have what it takes to succeed and that when you make a decision, you'll ensure that your decision is true. It's time to make a true decision to put yourself on the path of success you've always wanted.

A relationship with your Super Self increases self-confidence. The more and more I have talked to my Super Self, I have seen that I do have the answers and that I can achieve the things I want to in my life. The more I have seen the right answers, the more right decisions I have made. It will increase your self-confidence. It will increase your ability to not second-guess yourself. It will increase your belief levels and make them so high that you will create a powerful and contagious persona around you. It will create a whole new you, and it will become you. What is happening with each new decision and with each bit of information you are getting from the Super Self is your Super Self is emerging from the inside out. It is coming into you, through the you that you are today.

The more you use your Super Self, the more it gets to shine through into your daily life. The person you are intended to comes out and people around you will notice. It's an amazing thing. You'll see it all around you. You'll see it within yourself. This technique is so easy, so simple, and yet it is so powerful. It's made a huge difference in my life. Make a true decision right now to make a change in your life. Couple that true decision with your Super Self, and you can achieve whatever "it" may be that you want to do.

By using these techniques and implementing them into your life, there is no doubt you will see a change. You will see growth in your life unlike you have ever seen before. Take the step forward and implement these into who you are and you can achieve the lifestyle that you have always dreamed of living. In the end, you are responsible for your own success. You have control over your life and you can make the true decision to change your life!

OPPORTUNITY MATRIX

When talking about opportunity, many people reference opportunity in the way that there is not enough of it. They don't see opportunity. They don't have the same opportunities as another person; therefore, they cannot have the success that another person has in whatever they choose to do.

Perhaps it's in losing weight. "I can't lose weight. I have to work a full-time job, so I don't have the opportunity like those people on TV to work out all day long and watch what I eat. I don't have the opportunity because I have a job in order to build my own business because I don't have the time available to do that.

"I don't have the opportunity to travel the world because I have a family, and I can't possibly take my family with me traveling the world. I don't have the opportunity to do whatever it may be." They are excuses.

We can equate opportunity in most people's vocabulary with the word excuse. That's a fact. When most people use the word opportunity, they're using it as an excuse, as the reason why they can't do something. They don't have enough of it even though they don't know what it is to start with, but they don't have enough of it. Therefore, they can't get or attain the goals they want to achieve.

What if that's the case? First, let's define what an opportunity is. According to the dictionary, an opportunity is a situation or condition favorable for the attainment of a goal.

Does that opportunity have to do with money? Most people also equate opportunity with financial means. Understand that it's not about money. It's about anything that you want to do in your life. There is opportunity all around you.

My focus in this chapter is to look at the opportunities you have, discover them, recognize them and then filter them. Even though you may be presented with an opportunity, it doesn't mean you should take advantage or use that opportunity.

The question comes down to; can we train ourselves to recognize opportunity? The answer is yes.

Recognize Opportunity

Opportunity is all around you all day long. "You don't know my life and what I'm going through." You're right. I don't know your life or what you're going through. I would dare to say sitting in front of you right now at any given point, there are 50–100 different opportunities except you don't recognize them. You don't understand what is happening around you.

The point is you need to recognize an opportunity and understand how it can benefit you one way or another. First, you need to realize how to look for an opportunity. Once you understand how to recognize one, you can take advantage of it.

The reason why it's hidden from you right now is the same reason why you don't notice most of the things happening around you right now. For example, have you ever noticed that when you buy a new car, the moment you drive off that car lot you notice every single same make, model and even color of car that is just like yours?

It's kind of strange. It's like magic where one minute you're blind to it and the next minute you see it all over the place. Why is that? Why does that happen?

There is something in our brain called the reticular activating system, and it creates awareness for specific things that you have in your consciousness. The classic example as I just mentioned is a car. You're driving down the road in your brand new car; it's a beautiful color; you love it.

Suddenly, you drive off the parking lot and you notice that every 10th car is that exact same car. Why didn't you notice it before? Because your reticular activating system wasn't activated; therefore, you didn't notice it.

When you understand this; it's the same thing that's preventing you from seeing the opportunities that surround you — you haven't activated your sense of awareness for seeing the opportunities. What it boils down to is that you just don't know what to look for.

This starts with a basic idea of what you want to achieve. Remember, you're not just talking about financial gain. It could be financial, spiritual, health or a number of different things you want to achieve in your life. Don't limit what the definition of opportunity is. Define what your goal is first. It could be anything you want to achieve.

Work Towards Your Goal

I'm going to talk about goals in a little bit different way than most people do. Most self-help books and courses will tell you the same thing about your goals. I want you to go a little further and write them in financial, spiritual and wealth categories.

Here's what others typically say…

- Post it some place where you can see it every day. Put it by your computer, on your window, on your dashboard, everywhere so you can see it and are constantly reminded of what this goal actually is, so you don't forget it.

- Then say your goals out loud three to four times a day, every day.

- Do that for 21 days in a row.

In doing this, you're supposed to be well on your way to achieving goals.

You may have attempted or tried things like this before. There is some validity to what that method is. It's the idea of writing down your goals, and I do believe you should have a written list of goals, but I believe in doing it a bit differently.

I believe you should write it down, understand what they are, but focus in on a specific task that you want to achieve on one of those goals. Have a specific time throughout the day where you work toward that goal.

For example, let's say you have a goal of losing weight. You can have the goal written down and you can post it on your mirror, your car, talk about how thin you are in a very positive way and act as if it already happened, but you know what? If you continue eating junk food and don't exercise, you're not going to lose weight. That is just how it's going to work. There has to be some action to take place to achieve anything that you want in life.

Do a little time out with me right now. Everyone wants something that is magical. We would like to believe that there is a secret somewhere that is being withheld from us, which is preventing us from attaining our place or function in life. It is one of those things that if we knew the secret, we too, could become one of the privileged. We too, could become that thin body on the beach that we see on television.

We too, could have a huge amount of wealth. We too, could have what our life's desire is. We want to believe that there is something out there that is mystical in nature that would help us do this, and it's just being withheld from us. The secret of the ages is just not within our grasp. We're not smart enough or don't hang around the right people in order to attain that.

That is not true. It boils down to action. You need to work toward what it is that you want a little each day. Part of the idea of reaching a goal is to act on it. You must put time in to get something out. There is no other way around it.

Yes, you can think positively about it. There is nothing wrong with that. Yes, you can write it down, but that in itself is not going to get you there. There must be an allotted amount of time put towards reaching that particular goal, no matter what it is.

It's like the old question that you hear, "How do I get to Carnegie Hall?" The answer is practice, practice, practice! That statement has been around probably since the early 1920s, but the fact is that it's true. You must continue to practice. You cannot become good at that which you don't practice. You cannot master a skill that you do not practice. **You cannot reach a goal which you do not put time toward.**

When you see something, what you need to understand is how it applies to you. Opportunity is nothing more than sensing patterns. Each day, we are bombarded with tons of information. From everybody you interact with to the media, television, radio, you are bombarded with a lot of information from the books you read, the articles, to things you see and things people say to you, the interactions that you have.

Pattern Thinking

There is so much information that is thrown at you. In order to help you consciously use this information, your brain filters out the vast majority of it. The brain can only understand a few items at the same time. Focus in on how you make opportunity from one of those items.

When you take all this information in, whether you know it or not, your brain is storing the information. That is how it works, but your brain senses patterns automatically. You are looking for things that are familiar to you amongst all of these patterns. Most people don't recognize the pattern scenario.

Pattern thinking is one of the keys to success. One of the greatest stories of pattern thinking is what I would refer to as the elite thinkers in our time. If you just look at our recent past in human history, people like Tesla, Einstein, Edison and Howard Hughes.

Howard Hughes was known to be a pattern thinker. He thought in images and patterns. He filtered information so he could find the patterns that would benefit him. He found the patterns, which were the opportunities in order for him to move or advance toward his ultimate goal, whatever it was at that time.

Your brain automatically senses patterns every day. It's looking for the patterns, the combinations, formations of information and you're just not recognizing what that information is because you're not looking for the opportunity in it. How can you start consciously forming patterns or looking for patterns? How can you bring the idea of using patterns more to your consciousness?

It starts with some basic exercises. What many people don't understand is that your brain, the way it thinks, is a muscle. The more you start using it in a different way, the stronger it will become. You will use that functionality even more, so you can learn different things in a different way.

One of the most basic things you can do, and it's even better, it's even enjoyable, is to find patterns. Take all the information you have and pull out a pattern, sensing or predicting the future in some way. How do you do that? You need to train for it, and I'll make your job extremely easy by telling you how to do it.

Go outside and lie down. You can get into a lounge chair or in the grass in your back yard. Go to your favorite spot outside, some place where you can lie down and look at the sky. All you're going to do is look at clouds.

It doesn't sound very productive does it? It's probably very relaxing for you. I know it is for me. When you're watching clouds, what your brain instantaneously does is searches for patterns, formations. It can't help it because a cloud, in essence, means nothing.

When your brain looks at this, it can't sense it or understand that this is random, that there is no pattern to it, so the brain starts to create associations in the clouds. It says that looks like this, that looks like a horse, that looks like a bear, and that looks like a face, an eye, a nose, a dinosaur. It tries to justify what it's seeing, but what it's really doing is sensing patterns and formations.

The brain doesn't understand randomness. Look out your door, your window, go outside and stare at the sky. As the clouds pass by, you will start to see patterns, formations of what you are comfortable with, what you have seen before. It is searching through all of the information that you've acquired over your lifetime. It's like going through an index card box. It's flipping through each one of the cards saying no, no, no, no, kind of looks like this, but not quite.

Then it's looking for the right card that is going to match up with that cloud; many times it can't find it, so it moves on. It goes to the next section and next section until it finds something that it is justified by, meaning it finds something that it can see, and it recognizes that makes sense to it.

How do clouds relate to us seeing and identifying opportunities? It's an exercise in getting you used to seeing patterns. I'm going to tell you that I can't look at a cloud formation without trying to see something in the cloud. It's just something can't be helped.

The way this relates to the opportunities around us is it allows the brain to function in a way that will make sense of chaos. All the information that you take in every day is, in some ways, chaotic. There is no sense to it.

When your brain starts focusing on creating formations and looking for patterns, it will start to notice things around you. Last week, I saw this and this week I saw this and a few minutes ago I saw this and that is a pattern. You don't actually stop and say, "Hey, that's a pattern," but your brain starts recognizing and says this is something I should be aware of.

What does this relate to in the past? It will bring that thought or memory back up. Then it starts looking for combinations. It's like a lock; it starts looking for combination. If you combine this information, this information and this information, then it should logically mean this. That is what happens when you see opportunities.

Look for Opportunities

For example, I've spent much of my life looking for financial opportunities. I think everyone has been in situations like that where you've looked for an opportunity, but you just couldn't see it. As I write this, I'm sitting at my desk looking around at the things on it. I'm going to describe to you different opportunities that I have sitting on my desk.

I have a soda bottle. What is the opportunity I have with the soda bottle? What is it made of? Plastic. The first thing I could say that there is an opportunity in plastic recycling, simple enough. If I chose to go with that; that would be one financial opportunity associated with that.

I notice there is a label on the bottle. How can that be an opportunity? I could put advertising on that label. Maybe I could create a company and sell advertising on that particular label.

This particular soda bottle is empty, therefore it's warm. Maybe I can create some kind of a beer koozie where it slips over the top to keep your beer cold, maybe I can create something like that for soda; that would be easy.

I could have more than one different kind of soda so I could create multiple koozies to fit different types of brands for that. And, I could give them away for free. Why? Because I could put advertising on them.

Another thing sitting on my desk is a baseball hat. What could I do with a baseball hat? My hat is a Disney baseball hat. It has a Disney logo, an image of Mickey Mouse, and it's red; a very typical baseball hat.

How can I use this to my advantage? I could create a baseball cap for a town. I would go to the mayor of the town or figure out ways to raise money for the town — a fundraiser. I'd create a logo specifically for each individual city or town and then have it embroidered on different types of baseball hats. Then I would go around to residents and sell these baseball hats.

I could have the town sell it through the various city organizations and events. I could put a big advertisement in the newspaper saying this is going to raise money to do this for the town, fix up the local park or whatever it may be. I am going to create an identifying insignia for each individual town and then sell the baseball hats to do that.

Do you see my point? I'm just rattling off ideas that instantly come with this. What else do I have? I have a couple of screws on my desk because I just put my desk together. Maybe there's a better way to keep screws together.

Here's something odd. One of the greatest ideas I've ever seen as far as making money happens over and over again, throughout the years and that is taking something simple and repurposing it. There are these screws sitting here, and I know that the best way to keep screws together is with a magnet. That is easy.

What if we created a unique shaped magnet that would be memorable, hard to lose, and we could put screws on it. What if we could create a cool name for it? What if we made a magnet the way everyone envisions a magnet?

One of the things people envision about a magnet is that it's like a horseshoe shaped red with white tips on it. Maybe I can create a big magnet like that because that's what a lot of people envision; I could create a retro magnet. That would be an idea.

I see some cords. I just put in a phone system, so I have cords everywhere. Maybe it's another way that I could put cords underneath the desk to keep it out of the way of people's feet. People would certainly want that.

My computer is sitting here; there is some dust on my computer right now. Is there a better way for me to clean my computer? Is there a cleaning solution that can be designed for cleaning computer screens? Is there a cloth? What if there was a way that I could combine those two things together? That would be an opportunity, of course.

I have a book on my desk. Most people have a bookshelf or someplace where they can store their books, but most people don't have a bookshelf on their desk. What if I made a bookshelf for a desk? That would be cool. I would love to have a bookshelf on my desk.

What if I created a bookshelf and put them into a drawer? What if I made an actual leaning bookshelf so I could take a file cabinet drawer and sit my books inside of there? I could have a file cabinet drawer where I could easily access my books, see the spines, etc. That would be another simple idea.

I also have plastic bags that you get from the grocery and drug stores in my office. I have a couple of those. What if I went into a major chain like a Costco, Walgreen's or some national chain and said, "You are spending about a million dollars a year in bags. I would like to provide all your bags for free. We'll put your logo on the front of it, but I'd also like to put advertising on the back of the bag.

"I'll save you a million dollars a year just in your bag purchases alone. It's still going to have your branding and will be identical in every way, shape and form from the front of what you have right now; the exception is on the back, I'm going to put coupons from three or four local advertisers in the area."

How could they say no to that?

That's one of those business ideas I'm thinking I could probably do. This is what you do when you start thinking about things. I didn't even go through my entire office yet, but my point is there is opportunity all around you. If you recognize it, doing things like what I just did, I focused on one thing, the opportunity I was looking for on financial aspects.

I could go through each and every one of these pieces and look at them again except with a different twist. If I wanted a health aspect, I could look at the same item from a health point of view and come up with a bunch of different ideas, but you must be able to recognize the opportunity first.

Attaining Your Goals

When you see something, here is the path you need to go through.

- Start with a goal you want to attain.
- Ask yourself three questions.

When you first start with a goal, your brain starts tuning in towards that goal — that is step one. Step two is, as a result, of tuning into that goal, your brain will start to pick up patterns once you've trained it to. Now the brain will start noticing patterns happening around you in relationship to that goal.

The three questions you need to ask yourself are:

1. Does this pertain to me?
2. Can this help me become closer or get closer to my goal?
3. Is this something I can see myself doing?

This pattern is usually an opportunity. Is this specific or relevant to my goal at hand? Yes or no. If it's yes, move on to number two. Can this help me get closer to my goal?

It's very important because remember, the definition of an opportunity is a situation or condition favorable for attainment of a goal. If it doesn't help you become closer to your goal, then maybe you should say no to that opportunity. An opportunity has two different outcomes. It's either yes, this is for me; no, this is not for me.

Many times, you're presented with an opportunity that does pertain to you, that does bring you closer to your goals, but you can't envision yourself doing that or taking advantage of that. If you can't envision it, if you can't see yourself doing it, then it's another dead end, so you can't move on.

These three questions are how we recognize or filter out the opportunity, the first stage. If your answer is yes to all three of those then you would move on to the next step which is actually the matrix itself.

Start with a goal. As a result of the goal, you start seeing patterns and noticing similarities. These bring up opportunities for you. From there, you ask the three questions.

Does this opportunity pertain to me because I see opportunity every day? Yes, I can see the opportunity around it or the potential around it, but does this pertain to me? In most cases, no, it doesn't.

Does it help me get any closer to my goals? In some ways yes, but is it something I can see myself doing? Most of the things I could not see myself doing. There were hindrances, other factors that I would not want to do. There were one or two of the ideas I could get behind. It would be a great business model from a financial standpoint.

Once you've identified the opportunities that exist around you every day, the dilemma is choosing and acting upon the right ones. That is the problem.

You may be thinking that is a good problem to have, and you're right. Choices are a good thing. What you do at this point is filter one more, but this time you use what's called the actual opportunity matrix. The opportunity matrix is a filtering or sorting system that I created a long time ago.

Here is how it works. Opportunities are ideas with potential. We have to filter these down further to discover which one of these opportunities you should act first, second, or third on. This is how you do it.

Get out a sheet of paper and make four columns. Sometimes you'll use three columns and sometimes you'll use four. Let me explain. You're going to take your top ideas or opportunities and sort them in four different ways to find out which is the one that is best for you.

What's best for me may not be best for you.

Take a piece of paper long ways and draw four columns. You can use this with any number of opportunities but it's usually going to work best with six or seven "maybe" opportunities. If you have more, you'll have to do it again, but start with six or seven opportunities or ideas you may have.

The first column is only used if it is a **financial opportunity**. Take every one of your ideas or opportunities and list them down in the order of what could be the most profitable to what you feel would be the least profitable. Write your ideas in order. Most profitable at the top and the last would be the least profitable.

The next column is called **ease**. How easily can you do this or take advantage of this opportunity? Structure your list according to what could be accomplished the easiest to the hardest. Take the same opportunities in column number one but re-sort them in this column.

The next column is **time.** We sort the list according to time investment, which requires the least amount of time at the top down through the most amount of time at the bottom. Use the same items, reordered according to time.

The fourth column is **knowledge**. Which requires the least amount of new knowledge to the most amount of new knowledge? Least amount knowledge, meaning you don't have to go out and acquire a lot more information than you already know to the most amount of new knowledge at the bottom.

If you take your list of six or seven and put them into a chart like this, then you are looking for a common opportunity. An opportunity that is in the upper portion, say the top four positions. Is there an opportunity or an idea in the top four positions?

Compare column 1 to column 2. Is there an opportunity in the top four positions in column 1 and column 2? Is there an opportunity in column 1 and 2 that's also in column 3 in the top four positions? For column 4, is there an opportunity in all previous columns in the top four positions that is also in the top four position of column 4?

You're going to find maybe one or two ideas that are in the upper portion. What if you have different ones in each position? It depends. Which one ranks higher in each one of those four spots and that would be the one you would start with. What you want to do when it comes to a financial opportunity is to discover what is profitable for you, which is easy, doesn't take a lot of time, and you don't have to go out and gain a lot of knowledge to take advantage of it. That is a financial opportunity.

Let's say you were evaluating ideas or opportunities to allow you to become healthier or lose weight or something of that nature. You would remove the first column, of course. You would then look at how easy it would be to do, how much time will it take, how much new knowledge will you need to use to accomplish it?

Again, same process but we only use three columns instead of four. Four columns are only used if it's a financial opportunity. The other three columns are used in any other version of this. This is the opportunity matrix, and this is how you solidify your ideas and start recognizing opportunities.

Once you activate the reticular activating system for an opportunity to look for formations or patterns, at that point, you go through those first three questions. That is your first filter.

Then, you have a list of opportunities that will have passed the first test. Now what do you do? Now, list them. You know they all apply to you and they're all things that will help you get closer to your goal, and you can see yourself doing it. Now, you need to filter them one more time and this is where the opportunity matrix comes in.

It's a chart that helps you establish which goals, ideas and opportunities you should start working on first. When you recognize that, you can start putting everything into place. This brings us to the idea of implementation.

Implementation is King

Every idea or opportunity in its basic form is potential. Potential is a good thing, and it can also be a bad thing because it can be wasted as much as it can be used. If you're wasting it, you'll never get closer to whatever it is you want to accomplish.

All of these ideas have potential to help you move towards and achieve that goal. What you need to do is take action and implement the idea as quickly as possible. The faster an idea is implemented, the more likely you will be to achieve it.

A great example is cleaning your garage. Many people have great intentions on a Saturday afternoon to start cleaning their garage. If you have a garage, I think you can appreciate the fact that as soon as you start to clean it, something will happen. The phone will ring, and you'll talk to somebody, but then you'll get back to work.

Suddenly, something else will happen. The kids need to be taken to a friend's house, so you have to stop again. An unexpected friend will drop by, so you have to stop again. The more the process is dragged out, the less likely you are to finish cleaning that garage.

It's the same thing with an opportunity or idea. The longer it takes for you to go from idea to fruition, the less likely you are to succeed. The most excitement is at the moment of the inception of that idea.

As time goes on, that excitement wears off. Each passing moment, hour, day brings you further and further away from bringing that idea to fruition. Along with the idea of recognizing opportunity and training your brain to see the opportunities around you at any given moment in time and then to filter and even go through the opportunity matrix, the last piece, in order to make it work is implementation.

If you want to overcome procrastination, you do that with implementation and action. By doing that, it's going to put you on the fast track to success in anything you want to achieve.

A classic example of this, and I've seen many people do this time and time again, is when people try to lose weight. The procrastination is endless; it's Saturday, and you've made the decision to start your diet on Monday; you'll decide that as soon as the holidays are finished, you're going to start that diet; as soon as our vacation is over, I'm going to start that diet; as soon as my kids graduate, I am going to start that diet.

There are a ton of excuses that can be used to procrastinate on. Don't wait to try to implement any opportunity you are given. The longer it takes for you to do it, the longer you wait to implement it, the more the odds are going to go against you. I said it before, but it's worth repeating so you don't forget; every great opportunity is just potential unless you implement those ideas of that opportunity and start doing it as quickly as possible.

EPILOGUE

Congratulations and thank you on taking the next step of your journey to improving your life. Although, you're at the end of this book, remember you're now at the beginning of an incredible lifetime of achievements and accomplishments. This is by no means the end.

I ended the last chapter with the importance of implementation. It is the long lost key to achieving success beyond your wildest dreams. Where many people have failed, the people who have achieved extraordinary success utilized implementation as their springboard to accomplishing the impossible.

The world's knowledge is absolutely useless. It is just potential — potential ideas, wealth, achievement and accomplishments. That is, unless you put this information to use. Implementation allows you to unleash the floodgates of creativity and knowledge, which is pent up inside of you. I suggest you do not wait to start. The longer you wait, the less likely are to succeed.

Many times, life gets in the way unless you get in the way of life. Remember the garage story I just talked about? Your intentions are good, and you want to get the job done. Then life happens. With each interruption, your chances of cleaning that garage greatly diminishes. Don't let that garage be a symbol of your life. Implement the techniques that I've outlined in this book as soon as you can.

You are greatness. You possess unlimited potential. You can achieve anything you want in life. You only need to unleash your true potential by implementing what you've learned.

One last thought to always remember... Success Leaves Traces

ABOUT THE AUTHOR

Using the same techniques and strategies he teaches in *Success Leaves Traces*, Armand Morin has built a burgeoning international business, comprised of a multitude of software products, training programs, and sold-out events that have literally transformed the lives of hundreds of thousands of people all across the world and from all walks of life.

Go to Google and type in "Armand Morin." Now, go to Yahoo and do the same search. And finally, do the same search on MSN's Bing.

You'll find that his name alone is on over 3,000,000+ websites.

Armand is an author, self-made multimillionaire, and a top 100 Billboard recording artist and is one of the most well-known Internet marketers in the world today. Having started online in 1996, his personal businesses alone have generated hundreds of millions in online revenue. This doesn't include the millions of dollars his students have produced from his teachings.

Today, he's one of the world's most in-demand speakers, he trains people around the world and often shares the stage with the likes of Mark Victor Hansen (co-author of the *Chicken Soup For The Soul*® series), Jay Abraham, Loral Langemeier, T. Harv Eker, Les Brown, Robert Allen, just to name a few.

CPSIA information can be obtained
at www.ICGtesting.com
Printed in the USA
JSHW021144110620
6174JS00003B/47